CW01019428

Othello's Sacrifice

Essay Series 28

John O'Meara

Othello's Sacrifice

Essays on Shakespeare
and Romantic Tradition

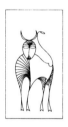

Guernica

Toronto / New York / Lancaster
1996

Typeset in Galliard by Calista Del Paese, Toronto.
The Publisher gratefully acknowledges support from
The Canada Council and The Ontario Arts Council.

Antonio D'Alfonso, Editor.
Guernica Editions Inc.
P.O. Box 117, Station P, Toronto (ON), Canada M5S 2S6
250 Sonwil Drive, Buffalo N.Y. 14225 U.S.A.
Gazelle, Falcon House, Queen Square, Lancaster LA1 1RN U.K.

Part One of this volume has appeared in print before in
English Language Notes, Vol. 28, No. 1, September, 1990.

Legal Deposit — Third Quarter
National Library of Canada
Library of Congress Catalog Card Number: 95-81892

Canadian Cataloguing in Publication Data
O'Meara, John, 1953 -
Othello's sacrifice: essays on Shakespeare and Romantic tradition
(Essay series ; 28)
ISBN 1-55071-040-0
1. Shakespeare, William, 1564-1616 — Criticism and
interpretation.
2. Tragedy. 3. Anthroposophy. 4. Steiner, Rudolf, 1861-1925.
I. Title. II. Series: Essay series (Toronto, Ont.) ; 28
PR2983.O44 1996 822.3'3 C95-920996-4
96 97 98 99 5 4 3 2 1

Contents

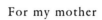

For my mother

Acknowledgments

I record my thanks to Charles Forker and to D.J. Palmer for their support and encouragement in the case of Part One and Part Two of this book, and to Arthur Kinney and the editorial staff of *English Literary Renaissance* for their feedback and suggestions when Part Three was being prepared, though no doubt all will be astonished to discover who that Messiah is to whom I play John the Baptist.

My special thanks and gratitude also to Nicholas Brooke for (unconsciously) pointing the way. He too will be astonished to discover where I believe his own insight was leading him. His superior honesty and integrity as a critic, not to mention his superb influence as a man ('I shall not look upon his like again'), never did get the full recognition these qualities deserved.

In still more personal terms, I acknowledge the continued and continuing support of Luigi Luzio and, of course, Antonio D'Alfonso, Society members, and Line.

We let Isaac actually be sacrificed.

Introductory

Shakespearean Tragedy as Negation

The tendency to want to romanticize Shakespearean tragedy, as well as the tendency to suppose that, if anywhere, it is in Shakespeare that tragic passion is brought under control, will no doubt continue to remain with us. They will do so primarily because we recognize that Shakespeare himself introduces these notions into his representations. This is quite apart from the unconscious power that the Romantic tradition also continues to exercise over us.

Love does not triumph over all only because we choose to continue to believe in the forms of love we have always known and wish to see it romanticized that way. Nor is there any hope in thinking that even the formal power of Shakespeare could bring the unconscious processes of tragedy into the complete light of day.

To put it in these terms is to paint a picture of the import of Shakespeare's development from a position well into his great tragic period. We need to recognize that Shakespeare had by then brought himself to the point of the complete *negation of all saving notions* in those familiar forms as they have come down to us to this day. Nor is it in the will of either the hero *or* the author to say how the renunciation will take place.

But it is also a case of seeing just how painfully tragic the process of renunciation is. It is a process that is being lived through immediately, and that we ourselves participate in directly. We do so by re-living the extraordinary way in which an attachment to these saving notions persists, even though the whole direction of experience is moving inexorably towards their negation.

Yet none of this explains how, or why, in Shakespeare's last phase, in spite of the great process of negation that has absorbed him down to that point, we suddenly get a miraculous recrudescence of otherworldly, salvific and romantic terms. Here entirely unfamiliar forms demand from us an altogether new way of perceiving.

Shakespeare's terms in the late romances also lie beyond the scope of formal representation. A further, evolutionary experience finally works directly *through* the tragedy that represents all life as death.

And that experience, as we shall see, is only fully confirmed for us as experience in the end *outside* the sphere of literature, in what is known today as *Anthroposophy,* which Rudolf Steiner helped to establish.

The essays brought together here follow on a previous study of mine (also published by Guernica) entitled *Otherworldly Hamlet*. In that volume, I focus on Shakespeare's absorption in a pattern of tragic alienation from traditional otherworldly and salvational motives of action.

In the present volume, I bring forward evidence of Shakespeare's absorption in a pattern of alienation from romantic-transcendental and formal-aesthetic solutions to tragedy, two other popular 'saving' notions that remain strong with us to this day.

Part One

Othello's Sacrifice as Dialectic of Faith: The Romantic-Transcendental Solution

It is the cause, it is the cause, my soul;
Let me not name it to you, you chaste stars,
It is the cause. Yet I'll not shed her blood,
Nor scar that whiter skin of hers than snow,
And smooth as monumental alabaster.
Yet she must die, else she'll betray more men.
Put out the light, and then put out the light:
If I quench thee, thou flaming minister,
I can again thy former light restore,
Should I repent me; but once put out thy light,
Thou cunning'st pattern of excelling nature,
I know not where is that Promethean heat
That can thy light relume. When I have pluck'd thy rose
I cannot give it vital growth again,
It needs must wither. I'll smell thee on the tree.
        [*Kisses her.*]

O balmy breath, that doth almost persuade
Justice herself to break her sword! One more, one more.
Be thus when thou art dead, and I will kill thee
And love thee after. One more, and that's the last.
So sweet was ne'er so fatal. I must weep,
But they are cruel tears. This sorrow's heavenly,
It strikes where it doth love. She wakes.

                                    (V.ii.1-22)[1]

Just because Othello's decision to kill Desdemona has become, at a certain point, irreversible and absolute, Othello cannot now stop himself from *again* valuing her with that characteristic immediacy and abandon with which he had always valued her. To view Othello's intention to kill Desdemona as separate from her in *any* sense (however favorably we may conceive of that relationship) is bound to distort the dreadful pathos of the tragedy — whether we think of Othello in 'the role of a god who chastises where he loves', or 'of a priest who must present a perfect victim'.[2] We must think of Othello as disposed to killing Desdemona, paradoxically, in tragically sublime identification with her life.

That identification, reinforced as it is by his sensuously kissing Desdemona three times, involves Othello ultimately in a tremendous intensification of anguish. In the philosophical sense, we must term this anguish absurd, since it has no reasonable limit whatsoever. Othello goes so far as to say, or desire to say, right through the unshakable resolution to kill Desdemona: 'I nevertheless believe that I shall get her':

> Be thus when thou art dead, and I will kill thee
> And love thee after.

(V.ii.18-19)

We may feel that all Othello is expressing here is an intense form of wishful thinking. Othello, we will feel, is not really thinking this thought through and could not begin to believe what his words literally imply. He is simply giving us a projection of his desire, basing himself on the familiar conceit of sleep as the counterfeit of death (suddenly given a spectacular poignancy and relevance in context).

Othello is, of course, only too aware in this speech of the absolute finality of death, and thus of the incommensurability of death and sleep. But to say that he is only aware of this truth, or that it is something he simply accepts, is to fail to enter into the drama, to see what it must mean for Othello to have to deal death to Desdemona as he has known her.

The intention attributed to Othello of seeking Desdemona's death 'to save her from herself, to restore meaning to her beauty'[3] grossly ignores the fact that, for Othello, Desdemona dead is meaningless. Othello's anguish is the more insufferable, especially now that *his love for Desdemona has once again be freed*, just because the resolution to put her to death settles the problem of her 'guilt'.

Condemned to death, Desdemona has now ceased to be guilty; and the further issue arises: 'how is Desdemona's death to be reconciled with that characteristically immediate love that is now once again freed in Othello, a love by nature entirely bound up with Desdemona's life?'

It is from this more evolved and transformed point of view that we finally enter, in imagination, into the dreadfulness of what Othello 'must' do. Suddenly struck by the likeness of Othello's case to that of the sublime-pathetic figure of Abraham, we let Kierkegaard interpret him for us:

> We let Isaac actually be sacrificed. Abraham had faith. His faith was not that he should be happy sometime in the hereafter, but that he should find blessed happiness here in this world. God could give him a new Isaac, bring the sacrificial offer back to life. He believed on the strength of the absurd, for all human calculation had long since been suspended(...)

> Let us now have the knight of faith make his appearance... he infinitely renounces the claim to the love which is the content of his life; he is reconciled in pain; but then comes the marvel, he makes one more movement, more wonderful than anything else, for he says 'I nevertheless believe that I shall get her, namely on the strength of the absurd.'[4]

It was Kierkegaard's mockingly triumphant view that the sublime dialectic of faith he had hit upon in the case of Abraham was the only dilemma Shakespeare had never ventured to speak about.[5] Yet here, for once, Kierkegaard's judgment would seem to have proved wrong, for this dialectic would seem to be precisely the one which Shakespeare glances at in *Othello*. Faced with the absolutely contradictory claims of death and of life, Othello inherits a dilemma and an anguish that could only be resolved ultimately in the manner of Abraham with whom Othello appears to be conceptually linked.

The sudden emergence of the Abraham-conception from the midst of Othello's tragic experience will be conditioned, of course, by our knowledge of the tragic irony of Othello's case. It will remain to decide Othello's actual relation to this suddenly invoked likeness.

But we could hardly imagine a potentially more dramatic *coup de théâtre*. An invocation of the possibility of a turn of events such as that associated with the Abraham story would seem to be a measure of the power of love developing in Othello.

Of course there could be no question in the world of *Othello* of a direct intervention from heaven. But this circumstance would almost seem to cast the audience itself in the role of the angel in the Abraham story, the Abraham-conception appealing, as it does, to a condition we have borne throughout the play by hovering over these thwarted lovers with our superior knowledge. That we know we would not intervene could only heighten the psychological intensity of Othello's anguish for us; and that heightening paradoxically draws us into still more immediate relation to an ultimate resolution, breeding in us a feeling that perhaps something might yet come to pass to interrupt the course of events as Desdemona suddenly awakes from sleep and death.

It is an illuminating experience, if initially a somewhat oblique one, to look back over Othello's speech and to see Othello as Abraham, except for the fact that Othello would kill Desdemona because he thinks she is guilty, except, that is, for the one line (l. 6) in which the fact is recorded, except also for the early reference to 'chaste'. Simply on the basis of that extraordinary note of sublime elevation sounded at the beginning, the Othello of the opening could hardly be thought unworthy of the comparison:

> It is the cause, it is the cause, my soul.

The Promethean aspect of the meditation (in l.12), which arises so naturally in this sublime context, would of course be also out of place, characteristically expressive as it is of counter-Renaissance 'metaphysical ache' or the denial of limit. [6] But, however small, there are those intensely poetic touches — of 'rose' and 'tree' — that might well suggest the symbolic Biblical landscape of the Abraham story, containing in themselves also that typological foreshadowing of Christ with whom, in line with Renaissance exegesis of the Bible, it would be only too easy to associate Isaac and Desdemona in their innocence.

Even the possibility of comparison with the Abraham-Isaac story on a sensuous plane is an experience for which an Elizabethan audience would have had an immediate precedent. They would have been adequately prepared for that experience in the Brome representation of the sacrifice from the mystery cycle of plays that had, not so long before, been a current feature of the popular life.[7] What this wonderfully humanized, and in its own way intensely moving, version would certainly have brought to the forefront in popular imagination is a feeling for the pathos and cost of the sacrifice, accentuated by Abraham's kissing Isaac clearly in the terms of sensuous life:

> A, Isaac, Isaac, son, up thow stond,
> Thy fayere swete mowthe that I may kis.
>
> (II.217-218)

> A, Isaac, my owyn swete child,
> Yit kisse me agen upon this hill!!
>
> (II.236-237)

Then there are the lines, to which I have given some attention, that clinch the comparison on the level of the story's dialectic:

> Be thus when thou art dead, and I will kill thee
> And love thee after.

And as we absorb the end of Othello's speech, the likeness to what might have inspired Abraham's own feeling would seem to present no difficulty at all:

> So sweet was ne'er so fatal. I must weep,

> But they are cruel tears. This sorrow's heavenly,
> It strikes where it does love.

A case might indeed be made for Shakespeare's perhaps deliberately weaving the Abraham-conception into Othello's situation as an irresistible development of the sublime pitch and direction of Othello's address to the sleeping Desdemona. Here, then, is the unconscious significance of the intention, well-noted of Othello in this scene, of sublime 'sacrifice'. What the implied likeness with Abraham would seem to signify in the end is Kierkegaard's own transcendental 'movement' of the spirit. The author appeals directly to the unhappy sense we have of the inevitability of Desdemona's death at this late point in the drama.

However, when Desdemona awakes eventually to deny her guilt, the tenuous framework of Desdemona's innocence on which Othello has been building is ironically threatened with being shattered. The drama shifts drastically from one term to the other — from a potential resolution, by way of a dialectic of faith along Kierkegaardian lines, into the actual irony of the case, with which Othello has to deal from this point onwards.

Caught as we are between these two terms over the course of a scene that Dr. Johnson thought too 'dreadful' to be 'endured',[8] we are not spared any measure of 'fear and trembling'. Both in Kierkegaard's sense, and also in a sense, beyond Kierkegaard, characteristic of Shakespearean tragedy.

It is clear that for Shakespeare, faced with the prospect of a transcendental resolution, it is the tragic experience which takes precedence, the unconscious process over which Shakespeare's characters are unable to exercise control and of which they fail to establish any conscious understanding.

In sharpest contrast with the extraordinary hope that has been invoked, we are suddenly made aware of the brutally ironical path along which even the most sublime effort of resolution is borne.

21

Indeed, what we are made to witness in the end is the furthest thing from the Abraham-conception: brute 'murder' rather than 'sacrifice'.

The most horribly ironical of deaths is experienced by one at the hands of the other of this most noble-minded of pairs:

> Des. Alas, he [Cassio] is betray'd and I undone!
> Oth. Out, strumpet! weep'st thou for him
>   to my face?
> Des. O, banish me, my lord, but kill me not!
> Oth. Down, strumpet!
> Des. Kill me to-morrow, let me live to-night!
> Oth. Nay, [an'] you strive —
> Des. But half an hour!
> Oth. Being done, there is no pause.
> Des. But while I say one prayer!
> Oth. It is too late. [*Smothers her.*]
> Des. O Lord, Lord, Lord!

(V.ii.76-84)

Part Two

Shakespearean Tragic Representation and The Formal-Aesthetic Solution

I

Again and again in the post-Romantic criticism of Shakespeare, one encounters a view that one suspects still haunts, in some repressed form or other, the minds of all students of the Bard. The view was expressed by Sidney Lanier, for instance, who helped to propagate it in *Shakespeare and His Forerunners*. There Lanier dug up the common ghost with an exuberance that became embarrassing to the twentieth-century reader: 'In Shakespeare,' Lanier intoned, 'passion is furnished with a tongue adequate to all its wants.'[9]

Bradley

After Lanier, passion was no longer regarded at least entirely as a question of character. For Bradley, who emerged directly out of the fashion which absorbed Lanier, 'the fundamental tragic trait' was indeed the 'tendency [in the hero] to identify the whole being with one interest, object, passion, or habit of mind'. But though this tendency illustrated 'the full power and reach of the soul', it linked up with the sense of an incomprehensible and uncontrollable 'force' (Bradley also called it 'fate').[10] This force was not only not strictly a property of character, it also received representation outside the character of the hero in the rest of the play.

Hough

Yet, in spite of the development toward greater sophistication in the understanding of passion, *the claim of full articulacy* survived. One finds it, for example, in Graham Hough's *A Preface to 'The Faerie Queene'*.

In his treatment of the full scope and possibilities of allegory, Hough considers the significance of 'incarnational literature'. Hough presents it as 'the kind of literature best represented by the work of Shakespeare.' 'Incarnational literature' is that in which 'any "abstract" content is completely absorbed in character and action and completely expressed by them.'[11]

Whatever Hough may have meant by 'abstract content', it was not strictly equatable with character inasmuch as it also encompassed 'action'. Equatable with neither one nor the other, it necessarily transcended both. It pointed, in fact, to an identity with the play as a whole and with the creating dramatist who shaped it.

'Abstract content', Hough associated, in fact, with 'theme', 'the moral-metaphysical abstract element', as distinguished from 'image', 'the concrete characters, actions, or objects in which it is embodied.'[12]

The sense of a consciously articulated and consciously elaborated 'theme' is enough to suggest that whatever Hough may have owed to Bradley for a perspective on drama that transcended character, he did not mean by 'abstract content' the sense of vast, unarticulated reserves of psychological-metaphysical energy evoked by Bradley's use of the word 'force'.

Leavis

By 'abstract content' Hough, it would seem, meant what F.R. Leavis meant when he said that 'the control over Shakespeare's words in *Macbeth*... is a complex dramatic theme vividly and profoundly realized'. For Leavis[13] its embodiment was, however, more narrowly a function of language, of 'the poetic use of language', or of 'poetry'. In Leavis, the emphasis was on 'poetry' as 'exploratory creation', or as Leavis' one-time associate, L.C. Knights, develops it[14], on 'a poetry that is profoundly exploratory, that evokes what it seeks to define'.

The emphasis on 'exploration' would seem at first to have encouraged a view that would see the chief value of the Shakespearean achievement in its tentative and, one presumes, by the way impressively successful, evocation of hitherto unarticulated areas of experience.

In fact, the emphasis in both men tended to enunciate a claim of full articulacy. Knights may have put it in less absolute terms. He seems to show an awareness of range of possible achievement that Leavis, in his essay on *Macbeth* at least, doesn't reflect on. There seems little question, however, of where the achievement was thought to lie. We are dealing in Shakespeare, according to Knights, 'with a poetry... in which the implicit evaluation of experience is entirely dependent on the fullness of evocation'. Leavis puts it more strongly: 'Poetry as creating what it presents, and as presenting something that stands there to speak for itself, or rather that isn't a matter of saying, but of being and enacting...'

G. Wilson Knight

To these views we may add G. Wilson Knight's emphasis on 'the visionary whole'[15] of a Shakespeare play. The term seems to have included for Knight what 'image' included for Hough — all the characters, actions, and objects in which the theme of a play is 'completely absorbed' and 'completely expressed', or embodied.

Whatever emphasis might be given to the aspect of suggestiveness in Shakespeare's achievement, and so, to a theme that remained finally *in*determinate however fully evoked, the effect in all these cases was to treat the achievement as if it were a *full articulacy*. As the very epitome of 'incarnational literature', Shakespeare was said to proceed by an 'harmonious wholeness' between theme and image that Hough himself denied, for example, to the term 'symbolism' where theme and image 'assert their unity, but the unity is never achieved, or if it is, it is only a unity of tension'.[16]

Apart from the passages in which it is the poetry that was believed to hold forth a power of full articulation, equally popular with critics were those in which an inchoate verse was thought to do so: for example, in Lady Macbeth's sleepwalking scene, and in Lear's mad scenes. Alwin Thaler once claimed that whereas Richard only talks about 'the unseen grief that swells with silence in the tortured soul'

> ...Lady Macbeth... really expresses it, in broken whispers which are the sighs of a soul unbosoming itself, at last, of long-repressed agonies.[17]

Writing in the mid-nineteenth century, J. Wilson, in the *Dies Borealis*, once justified considering Lady Macbeth's passage as prose rather than as the alternative blank verse, in similar terms; it must be in prose

> because these are the *ipsissima verba*, yea the escaping sighs and moans of the bared soul. There must be nothing, not even the thin and translucent veil of the verse, betwixt her soul showing itself, and yours beholding.[18]

Wilson's argument about the greater spiritual transparency of prose here is a spurious one, for no amount of formal 're-shuffling' of the form of Lady Macbeth's lines will prevent her 'prose' from hitting our ears as rough blank verse.

The idea of the bared soul is, as I argue below, especially misleading.

Writing in the middle of this century, W.H. Clemen had roughly the same thing to propose about the 'bared mind' in the case of Lear:

> The images of the next scenes [III.iv; III.vi] in which the King goes mad, are again illuminating for Lear's state of mind. The swiftly passing images, logically unconnected with each other, which we hear Lear utter, correspond to the abnormal state of the King; they are the adequate form of perception and expression of a lunatic. 'It is his mind which is laid bare,' Charles Lamb said as an interpretation of these strange speeches — especially in the fourth act. Lear's insanity should not be dismissed as simple craziness. It is rather another manner of perception, by means of which, however, Lear now sees and recognizes what formerly remained concealed to him, as long as he was sane. The images are the fragments of his inner visions, which have not yet attained to the form of thoughts; they

> have not yet been transformed, ordered and connected in logical sequence and in the service of clear statement.[19]

The quotation from Lamb follows rather perilously on the point about Lear's lunacy. It suggests an identity between the bared mind and mental fragmentation even more extreme than the one actually implied by Clemen in the passage as a whole. Just what Clemen means by his quotation from Lamb takes some unravelling to say. But judging by the ring of his use of the words 'interpretation' and 'strange', he seems to suggest a measure of bafflement in himself that could not surround the sort of claim implied by his reference. For no one's mind could be laid bare to one to whom that mind remained in any way or to any degree unknown.

Yet that Lear's 'fragments' remain to be logically connected or clearly stated establishes beyond doubt for Clemen that these 'visions' represent Lear's inner mind 'bared' to us.

Yet one would think it obvious that no manner of mental fragmentation could ever be mistaken for the vision whose actualization is by these devious means being aimed at. What has been taken for positive vision in Lear is actually the radically ambiguous creation of a mind lost to the violent consequence of a 'mere' identification with vision that has in fact become unreal.

It is precisely because one is bound to posit a disastrous *unreality* at the basis of the imagination of so many of Shakespeare's characters (as I shall show) that to speak of a representation of complete value, in the sense attributed to the Shakespearean achievement by post-Romantic criticism, seems to be finally quite unfounded.

The great value of the work undertaken by the critics mentioned, as well as many others, lies in having brought the twentieth-century reader that much closer to what Coleridge described as Shakespeare's characteristic achievement of 'making everything present to imagination'. But in vindicating this claim, these critics also went too far.

What is questionable is the *incarnational enthusiasm* which insinuates itself into what strikes one otherwise as a penetrating emphasis on the need for responding to the precise quality of the dramatic experience. The 'theme' of a Shakespearean drama cannot be grasped except as superb creation. But it is quite impossible to claim that the creation is brought to the point of an incarnational completeness.

The formal representation of passion in Shakespeare offers ample evidence for this general moral. In what follows, I offer a detailed analysis merely of one portion of this massive testimony. It shows the significant use that might be made of what turns out to be the profoundly problematic tenor of Shakespeare's representational creation. *Belying the post-Romantic claim of a full articulacy or representation of incarnational value.*

II

Among the literary conventions drawn upon for the formal representation of inward feeling, probably the most traditional and primitive but by no means the least effective, was the simple, straightforward statement testifying to feeling. The device took many forms and, as we shall see, came to acquire in Shakespeare a sophistication one would hardly have thought predictable from its apparent naivety as a representational formula.

The device of using a character forthrightly to inform the audience of his/her inward state of mind came to express far-ranging evocative levels and a great variety of emotional nuances. In *self-exposition*, a character could resort to a technique by which he/she described the inward feeling more particularly and extensively, thus accounting for the essential movement of the mind. Alternatively, the character could also allude to the seat of passion, either by a localizing gesture directed to the breast or the head, or simply and most often, by open, verbal reference to the heart.

Not all references to inward feeling of this kind have, of course, representational significance. Many references appear too casually in the exposition or the dialogue to merit attention. Still more have a purely informative function. Kent's previous confrontation with Lear, and the possibility that Timon's steward has returned to his abandoned master because it has been rumored that he is again wealthy, require that we know the genuineness of their intentions. When Kent returns to his own master, he is made to say 'So may it come, thy master, whom thou lov'st,/Shall find thee full of labors' (*Lear*, I.iv.6-7); likewise, Timon's steward: 'I will present/ My honest grief unto him' (*Tim.*, IV.iii. 469-470).

Other references with some representational significance are, nevertheless, primarily designed either to define the emotional effect of a scene, as in Horatio's reaction to the Ghost in *Hamlet*: 'It [harrows] me with fear and wonder' (I.i.44), or to signal a momentary intensification of the action, as in Claudius' reaction to the murder of Polonius: 'O, come away!/My soul is full of discord and dismay' (IV.i.44-45). Others may be used to redress or re-adjust the point of view, as in Aufidius' sudden change of mind at the end of *Coriolanus*: 'My rage is gone,/And I am struck with sorrow' (V.vi.146-147).

Aufidius' sentiment signals and consolidates the larger structural effort at the end of the play to re-emphasize Coriolanus' essential nobility, after still another, understandably ill-endured, display of anger on Coriolanus' part has sparked his murder. With this we may compare Bolingbroke's protestations towards the end of *Richard II*, which are put to an analogous use: 'Lords, I protest my soul is full of woe/That blood should sprinkle me to make me grow' (V.vi.45-46). The judgment redressed here is a far more complex one that includes Bolingbroke's own need to re-affirm himself as King in the face of the deeds committed.

The more prominently psychological implications of Bolingbroke's lines, however — Bolingbroke's sense of guilt and dread — demonstrate how the more broadly dramatic function of self-exposition could merge into a more explicitly representational function. The lines Claudius speaks in Hamlet just prior to the nunnery-scene also have that double function. For the first time we learn from Claudius himself of his responsibility for the murder of Hamlet's father: 'O, 'tis too true!/How smart a lash that speech doth give my conscience!' (III.i.48-49). The lines reinforce the vital information we have about the murder and they also represent Claudius' sudden inward qualm. They actually enact the inward motion the qualm entails — 'smart', 'lash', and 'speech' providing us with a concrete representation in the motion and burning effect of the whiplash.

The emotional process implied in Claudius' lines is a good indication of effective differences within the technique of self-exposition. These I shall get into later, when I consider the question of different possible levels of evocative representation.

The representational form of Bolingbroke's lines, to return to this, links them with a common self-expository device that consists in representing inward passion by the *protestation* or persuasion that it is being felt.

1. Protestation

The device is used again in the front end of the last scene of *Othello* when Desdemona suddenly realizes that Othello is serious about killing her: 'And yet I fear you.../ ...Why I should fear I know not,/Since guiltiness I know not; but yet I feel I fear' (V.ii.37-39). It recurs in *Antony and Cleopatra* where it represents Enobarbus' crushing sense of remorse when his master, whom he has deserted, repays his treachery with a gesture of magnanimity: 'I am alone the villain of the earth,/ And feel I am so most' (IV.vi.29-30).

Now it is not at all unusual in Shakespeare, particularly not in the later tragedies, to find several things being underlined by one and the same passage. This is exemplified in Desdemona's case where the self-exposition, besides reflecting the tragic force and influence of Othello's personality, expresses the depth and power of Desdemona's *intuition of tragic irony*. The intuition is of an extraordinary kind, comparable to Hermione's in *The Winter's Tale* when, faced with analogously mad charges from Leontes, the Queen remarks: 'There's some ill-planet reigns;/I must be patient, till the heavens look/With an aspect more favorable' (II.i.105-107).

What Desdemona intuits, less happily than Hermione, is not simply her own death but the whole fatal pattern behind it. This is a point made clear both to us and to herself in her reaction to Othello's disclosure of Cassio's supposed death a little later: 'O, my fear interprets' (V.ii.73). What the self-exposition serves to do in this case is to evoke *deeper* levels of emotional engagement in Desdemona, levels, moreover, that are indicated precisely *because* they arise mysteriously. It should be noted, too, that it is the mysteriousness of Desdemona's feeling that causes it to be ambiguously manifested to Othello as guilt, thus aggravating the tragic irony.

Emphasis on the tension between inward feeling and outward action and event seems to be the point consistently associated with protestation as a self-expository device, though the emphasis, as one would expect of Shakespeare, exists in different forms.

In Bolingbroke's case, protestation measures the immediate inadequacy of his remorse as amends for Richard's murder. It is the *magnitude of the crime* that at once forces and invalidates the protestation. One would expect to find the same sort of relation between feeling and event in the case of Enobarbus whose situation is clearly analogous. But there the self-exposition seems rather to measure the *inadequacy of all expression* for a remorse that is absolutely final.

In this effect, Enobarbus' case invites comparison with what is perhaps the most spectacular use in Shakespeare of this self-expository device. Towards the end of *Coriolanus*, Coriolanus' mother succeeds in breaking down Coriolanus' will outside the gates of Rome. She saves the city from his revenge but provokes from the hero the somewhat pathetic cry: 'But, for your son, believe it — O, believe it —/Most dangerously you have with him prevail'd,/If not most mortal to him' (V.iii.187-189).

Coriolanus' outcry here ends up being more unconscious posturing from pride, designed, it seems, to deflect from the sense of shame over his submission to his mother. Far from being 'mortal' to him (except, of course, in the ironic sense in which it incites Aufidius to conspire his death), the significance of the submission is soon forgotten. Coriolanus returns to Corioli claiming to be 'No more in-

fected with my country's love/ Than when I parted hence...'
(V.vi.71-72).

Just the same, at the time it is spoken, Coriolanus' outcry expresses a perfectly genuine sense of shame. What it
impresses upon us is, as with Enobarbus, the sense of an
undemonstrably inward feeling. What it also impresses upon
us is a sense of the general unruliness of inward feelings.
Feelings mysteriously elude Coriolanus just as they compul-
sively overcome him. However, in the recourse to the protestation of feeling, Coriolanus' outcry typifies one of the possible, if always inadequate, means available to the character
in his/her endeavor at inner representation. In the grapple
with the knowledge and expression of inward forces (elusive,
mysterious and extreme), he/she can, at least, emphasize or
underline that they are there.

2. Inner Evocation

Extensive efforts *are* made to lend greater and greater inwardness of feeling to the self-expository technique. This is
achieved particularly through verbal evocation.

As a result of verbal nuance, even a relatively naive
presentation of emotion can still project the suggestion of
inward depth (in 'too *far* gone') in York's 'O Richard! York
is too far gone with grief,/Or else he never would compare
between' (*Richard II*: II.i.184-185).

We may compare similar evocation in Leontes' 'Fie, fie,
no thought of him;/The very thought of my revenges *that
way*/Recoil upon me' (*The Winter's Tale*: II.iii.18-20). Expressed here is Leontes' frustrated desire to revenge himself
on Polixenes for the effect on Mamillius (Leontes falsely sup-

poses) of Hermione's 'dishonor'. Consider, also, Macbeth's 'Our fears in Banquo/ Stick *deep*' (*Mac.* III.i.48-49).

Verbal allusion to a *process, movement, or continuum of emotion* is, in fact, the secret to inner evocation in Shakespeare. It forms part of the basis for the uncanniness of such familiar lines as Banquo's 'Fears and scruples *shake* us' (*Mac.*, II.iii.129), or Angelo's 'And in my heart the strong and *swelling* evil/Of my conception' (*Meas.*, II.iv.6-7); Brabantio's 'Belief of it *oppresses* me already' (*Oth.*, I.i.143), or Lear's 'My wits *begin* to turn' (*Lr.*, III.ii.67).

The means by which an inward process is suggested are various and all the more fascinating. Brilliant effects are reaped from such small touches and familiar devices. In some cases, it implies the *substitution* of one part of speech for another. The substitution, for example, of the gerund for the noun, in the following line of the King's in *All's Well That Ends Well*: 'I am wrapp'd in dismal thinkings' (V.iii.128).

The culminating exploitation of gerundial form (though there is, of course, no alternative form of speech here) is Cleopatra's sublime 'I have /Immortal longings in me' (*Ant.*, V.ii.280-281). Cleopatra's statement also benefits from the ambiguity of a more poetic phrasing in which 'immortal' is conducive at once to the meaning 'longings for immortality' and the more intense 'longings that are immortal'.

In other cases, it is alliteration that is probed for effect. Antony's 'Love, I am full of lead' (*Ant.*, III.xi.72) manages to evoke with a brilliant concreteness the weight of Antony's despair simply by the sheer confluence of 'l' sounds towards the end of the line. It is by a similar touch, by a process of identity achieved in the verbal fusion of 'thought' and 'murther' in the 'th' sound, that Macbeth's thought of murder takes on a quality of reality, in the lines 'My thought, whose murther yet is but fantastical' (*Mac.*, I.iii.139).

In Lear's 'Thou art a soul in bliss, But I am bound/Upon a wheel of fire' (*Lear.*, IV.vii.45-46), it is the vowel sounds that are exploited. The long 'e' and 'i' sounds, in 'wheel' and 'fire', follow upon a series of short vowel sounds, managing to suggest the infinite reach of Lear's suffering. The horizontal and vertical movements, respectively of the 'e' and 'i' sounds, are clearly designed to suggest an experience spread out through all of space.

In still other instances, a process of emotion is suggested by devices that are either so hackneyed or so daring, it is a wonder they work so well. It is illuminating to remark how successfully Shakespeare redeems a device so parodiable in his own day as the antithesis, in the following lines from *Othello*: 'By the world,/I think my wife be honest, and think she is not;/I think that thou art just, and think thou art not' (III.iii.383-385).

Part of the success of the use of antithesis here lies in transposing its application from the pretentiously high rhetorical sphere of the earlier dramatic verse of the period to one more conceivably real. Shakespeare motivates its use by a movingly pathetic desperation. Nonetheless, the vacillating motion of doubt that the antithesis enacts is successfully rendered, above all, by the frank simplicity of the antithetical terms.

A comparably redeeming use of a naive rhetorical device is to be found in Macbeth's 'But now I am cabin'd, cribb'd, confin'd, bound in/To saucy doubts and fears' (*Mac.*, III.iv.23-24). Here redundancy is quite ingeniously made use of to suggest the unavailing inner struggle against inevitable spiritual circumscription.

On the one hand, Shakespeare achieves inner evocation by an ingenious use of often hackneyed devices. On the other hand, he achieves this by a competent use of devices at once bold and imaginative — in Angelo's 'This deed *unshapes* me quite, makes me unpregnant/And dull to all proceedings' (*Meas.*, IV.iv.20-21), and Othello's 'I tremble at it. Nature would not invest herself in such *shadowing* passion without some instruction' (*Oth.*, IV.i.39-41). Here, Shakespeare combines with an inner emotional process by *verbs of action* the suggestion of a process quite properly and appropriately inchoate (through a dark movement in the words 'unshapes' and 'shadowing').

These instances bring us closer to the literal knowledge of a character's inward experience. In other instances, Shakespeare is more daring still. In the romances, inward feeling is often represented by sharp, single *nouns of sensation*. There is, for example, the following representation of despair in Imogen over Posthumus' enforced, violently sudden departure from court: 'There cannot be a *pinch* in death/More sharp than this is' (*Cym.*, I.i.130-131); following this, there is her half-conscious response to her father's vituperative anger: 'I am senseless of your wrath; a *touch* more rare/Subdues all pangs, all fears' (*Cym.*, I.i.135-136).

We may compare with this Prospero's representation of Ariel's unnatural 'compassion' for Prospero's spell-bound victims: 'Hast thou, which art but air, a *touch*, a feeling/Of their afflictions' (*Tp.*, V.i.21-22), or the general representation in this play of conscience as inward 'pinching' (cf. V.i.74-77). It is a technique that can be ascribed to the characteristic presentation in the last plays of what have been called 'states of profound sensation'.[20]

But the identification of inward passion with sensation is a technique discernible incidentally in earlier plays. There is, for example, Troilus' 'I am giddy; expectation whirls me round;/Th' imaginary relish is so sweet/That it enchants my sense' (*Troil.*, III.ii.18-20). Here, Shakespeare combines again with the evocation of an inner action, in 'whirls', the quite extraordinary device of invoking in the audience those concrete sensations that every lover has known at one time or another on the verge of an assignation. It is by the same appeal to familiar sensations that in the major scene of confrontation between Othello and Desdemona (IV.ii) we are brought one step closer to the direct knowledge of the rankling grief Othello experiences in his jealousy, in two of the most heart-wrenching lines in all of *Othello*: 'O thou weed!/Who art so lovely fair and smell'st so sweet /That the sense aches at thee, would thou hadst never been born!' (IV.ii.67-69).

In all the instances of self-exposition quoted thus far, the underlying representational purpose is to fuse explicitness of representation on the one hand with inward actuality on the other.

All of the instances are to varying degrees explicit and actual in these senses. But behind the effort at inner evocation lies the attempt (superior to the plain protestation of feeling) to attach to the formal representation of passion a greater and more tangible inward actuality.

A third and more integrated device consists in attaching to the emotional actuality a more explicitly inward figure. Characters allude to the 'seat' of their passion by overt, verbal reference to the heart.

3. Overt Verbal Reference to the Heart

Reference to the heart as the seat of passion has more than a mere physical or physiological implication: it possesses simultaneously metaphorical and emotional implication; and it is all to the point that in this device the two are fused. The attempt at the direct, sensible representation of passion here takes the form of an effort to identify the two in the verbal figure. A very special one at that, one so ancient it has come to acquire a far greater inward concreteness for the human (and theatrical) imagination than the spoken word normally receives.

Instances of the use of verbal reference to the heart for purposes of the external representation of inward emotion abound. We shall only glance here at a few cases that are particularly illuminating. These exploit the device's singular expressive potentiality to suggest, at the same time, its inherent expressive limitations.

An early and comparatively primitive recourse to the device is to be found in Bolingbroke's 'I have too few to take my leave of you,/When the tongue's office should be prodigal/To breathe th'abundant dolor of the heart' (*Rd*. II, I.iii. 255-257). Bolingbroke speaks this as he prepares for exile, in answer to Gaunt's reproach for failing to return his friends' salutations. What Bolingbroke is saying is that he feels he must keep his words to express the grief entailed in being parted from his father. But implied in Bolingbroke's lines is that words could not adequately express this grief, the intensity of which is best represented for the moment by the phrase itself: 'th'abundant dolor of the heart.'

Recourse to verbal reference to the heart to express an emotion that could not otherwise be adequately represented is a recurrent representational focus. It crops up again in the following lines spoken by Richard where the phrase 'For on my heart they tread', apart from clarifying Richard's rhetorical figure, serves as a tentative reference to acknowledge the representational inadequacy of a desperate verbosity:

> Or I'll be buried in the king's high way,
> Some way of common trade, where subjects' feet
> May hourly trample on their sovereign's head;
> For on my heart they tread now whilst I live,
> And buried once, why not upon my head?
>
> (III.iii.155-159)

This feature also recurs in Brutus' 'That every like is not the same, O Caesar,/The heart of Brutus earns to think upon!' (*Caes.*, II.ii.128-129). The device provides Brutus with a tentative representational solution for the problem that faces both him and his author with regard to embodying his conflicting sympathies on the question of Caesar.

And finally, we may see it again in Antony's 'Triple-turn'd whore! 'tis thou/Hast sold me to this novice, and my heart/Makes only wars on thee' (*Ant.*, IV.xii.13-15). Here the device temporarily answers Antony's immediately unsatisfiable and ultimately unrelieved rage over Cleopatra's third purported piece of treachery.

A further aspect to the use of this device worth remarking on is the tendency, particularly in the later tragedies, to try to lend to it a greater naturalism and a deeper genuineness. An instance of this is to be found in Francisco's expression of melancholy at the beginning of *Hamlet*: 'For this relief much thanks. 'Tis bitter cold,/And I am sick at heart' (I.i.8-9). We may compare with this Macbeth's expression of despair and emptiness over the absence of love and loyalty in 'old age': 'Seyton! — I am sick at heart/When I behold —

Seyton, I say!' (*Mac.*, V.iii.19-20). Here the naturalism, if far more hurried in its effect, is considerably deepened.

Hamlet's famous profession of affection for Horatio is similarly a clear attempt to deepen the representational value of the ancient device: 'Give me that man/That is not passion's slave, and I will wear him/In my heart's core, ay, in my heart of heart,/As I do thee' (*Ham.*, III.ii.71-74). So too Desdemona's public profession of love for Othello: 'That I [did] love the Moor to live with him,/My downright violence, and storm of fortunes,/May trumpet to the world. My heart's subdu'd/Even to the very quality of my lord' (*Oth.*, I.iii.248-251).

Yet, as with the tentative representational significance of the earlier examples, the effort to deepen here clearly betrays an underlying sense that the device has its inherent representational limitations. Other devices in the genre of self-exposition generally attach to themselves, as we shall see, a disturbed sense of the gap between the external representation of passion that they provide and the actual inward nature and essence of the passion represented.

However, this is entirely in accord with the constant sense that, however serviceable, all devices are ultimately inadequate. At best they provide only a partial or technical solution to the forbidding challenge actually posed by the ideal of a literal representation of passion.

The duality between outward and inward reality that Shakespeare inevitably came up against is reflected dramatically in a fourth self-expository technique. Characters are made to refer to the seat or center of their passions, in this case along with an overt, localizing gesture.

4. Localizing Gestures to the Heart or the Head

It is a technique that, of course, might naturally accompany all references to the heart, or the head. But in certain cases this is an explicit feature of the reference; and its function then is clearly to suggest a physical or spatial locus for the inward passion. [21]

In some such cases, the device has an entirely ironic value dramatically emphasizing a serious gap in men's knowledge of themselves. It is clearly in all ignorance of the questionability of his cause, and more immediately of his ambiguously self-seeking motives, that Cassius, with a typical, histrionic imagination, insinuates his conspiratorial plans to Brutus in *Julius Caesar*: 'Then, Brutus, I have much mistook your passion,/By means whereof this breast of mine hath buried/Thoughts of great value, worthy cogitations' (I.ii.48-50).

It is in a somewhat lighter tone, but with implications no less serious for the matter of self-representation, that Troilus similarly, and with a comparable predilection for histrionics, aggrandizes his love-wounds in the opening scene of *Troilus and Cressida*: 'Call here my varlet, I'll unarm again./Why should I war without the walls of Troy,/That find such cruel battle here within?' (I.i.1-3).

In another case, the device, far from implicating human superficiality and emptiness, celebrates the inner-outer duality as the condition of human dignity. When facing Leontes' charges before an immediately acquiescent set of courtiers, cowed (or perhaps simply stunned for the moment) by his warnings against their intervention, Hermione disdains to express her grief outwardly:

> Good my lords,
> I am not prone to weeping, as our sex
> Commonly are, the want of which vain dew
> Perchance shall dry your pities; but I have
> That honorable grief lodg'd here which burns
> Worse than tears drown. Beseech you all, my lords,
> With thoughts so qualified as your charities
> Shall best instruct you, measure me.
>
> (*Wint.*, II.i.107-114).

The value attached to the duality here is typical of the return in the romances to a more discreet norm over the question of inward impenetrability. One resolves the problem of vindicating the reality of passion through a 'plain and holy innocence'.

But between the discreet resolution of the romances and the recognition of emptiness of the earlier plays stands the period of the later tragedies where the inner-outer duality and its immediate resolution are of the highest concern.

Instances in these plays measure at once the desire and effort to express, control or possess the inward passion in a literal sense, and at the same time the tragic helplessness of characters in this effort. In some of these instances, one feels that the desire is for a literal, physical possession of the inward passion.

When Lear, for example, violently strikes his head on first explicitly recognizing his folly in dispossessing Cordelia ('O Lear, Lear, Lear!/Beat at this gate, that let thy folly in/And thy dear judgment out!' (*Lr.*, I.iv.270-272)), it is more than an irreversible error that Lear underlines by his gesture. It is the tragic gap between the inner and the outer Lear, specifically the inaccessibly inward unruliness and in-dependency of his emotions. It is the very same gap — the *physical* distance between the inner and the outer man — that is resisted in a second such gesture by Lear in the storm: '[this] tempest in my mind/Doth from my senses take all feeling else,/Save what beats *there* — filial ingratitude!' (*Lear*, III.iv.12-14).

In other instances, the technique clearly constitutes a pathetically desperate alternative to being unable to express an *inexpressibly intense* and (from the others' point of view) an impenetrably inward *emotion*. Consider, in this connec-tion, Lear's complaint to Regan about Goneril's malice to-wards him: 'O Regan, she hath tied/Sharp-tooth'd unkind-ness, like a vulture, here. [*Points to his heart*]/I can scarce speak to thee; thou'lt not believe/With how deprav'd a quality' (*Lear, II.iv.134-137*). *Or Hamlet's movingly sudden, candid confiding to Horatio, on the verge of his duel with Laertes, of an innermost despair: 'Thou wouldst not think how ill all's here about my heart —'(Ham.*, V.ii. 212-213).

The helplessness of these characters before the control or possession of inward reality is perhaps most spectacularly demonstrated in another instance of the technique in *Othello*. In the process of bewailing the singular intolerability for him of suffering from betrayal, Othello suddenly points to Des-demona's breast as the locus of his suffering being, now en-tirely outside his control, in a most painfully tragic expression of the convention of the exchange of hearts:

> Yet could I bear that too, well, very well;
> But *there*, where I have garner'd up my heart,

> Where either I must live or bear no life;
> The fountain from the which my current runs,
> Or else dries up: to be discarded thence!
> Or keep it as a cestern for foul toads
> To knot and gender in! Turn thy complexion there,
> Patience, thou young and rose-lipp'd cherubin—
> I *here* look grim as hell!
>
> (IV.ii.56-65) [22]

Awkward, vexatious, is the transition from 'there' to 'here'. This can be explained, however, by the fact that in the interval Othello has moved towards Desdemona and is now face to face with her. Othello's tormented comments in the following lines about Desdemona's beauty and sweet smell clearly imply this (re: ll's 68-69). The stage action is itself representationally significant, a dramatically pathetic alternative to being unable to penetrate any further, ontologically — to Desdemona's heart.

Reflections of the inner-outer duality are likewise discernible in other instances of self-expository technique. In some cases, the suggestion of an inwardly withheld passion simply expresses a condition of social *isolation* in which the characters do not have or have not had the opportunity to express their emotions at all.

Hence, Marina's necessarily private knowledge of grief over her lost parents and her persecution by Dionyza as well as her period of stay at the brothel, till her meeting with Pericles: 'She speaks,/My lord, that, may be, hath endur'd a grief/Might equal yours, if both were justly weigh'd' (*Per.*, V.i.86-88).

Marina's purely expository account of her grief sub-
sequently, reflects once again the characteristically discreet
resolution of duality in the romances. Nowhere is this more
clearly evident than in other instances of self-exposition in
The Tempest. When Miranda temporarily withholds expressing her love for Ferdinand at their betrothal,

> Ferd. Wherefore weep you?
> Mira. At mine unworthiness, that dare not offer
>   What I desire to give...
>
> (III.i.76-78),

it is significant that the duality should be thought
reproachable rather than agonizing.

However, it is not only, as the cases of Miranda and
Marina imply, that the romances return to standards of 'plain
and holy innocence'. As the example of Hermione has testi-
fied, the privacy of inward life is here rendered a new respect
and sanctity. This attitude is further reflected in Prospero's
distant observation of the love between Ferdinand and Miranda: 'So glad of this as they I cannot be,/Who are surpris'd
[withal]; but my rejoicing/At nothing can be more.'
(III.i.92-94); also, in the lengthy, silent, private self-com-
muning permitted Gonzalo over the final reconciliations at
the end of the play: 'I have inly wept,/Or should have spoke
ere this.' (V.i.200-201)

In the tragedies, however, the inner-outer *duality* remains
consistently disturbing. It takes the form, in other cases of
self-exposition, of self-representations that because of one
form of *pride* or other, obscure, falsify or simply misrepresent

the inward feelings that the characters are actually experiencing. In these cases, what the characters present as their inward feelings is clearly belied by what we know from hints in the action to be what they actually feel.

This is clear, for example, when Alcibiades claims to pity Timon when they meet again in the woods, after Timon has rejected all human society — 'I am thy friend, and pity thee, dear Timon' (*Tim.*, IV.iii.98). It is not Timon whom Alcibiades actually pities, but himself whose own fate he sees in Timon's: 'I have heard, and griev'd,/How cursed Athens, mindless of thy worth,/Forgetting thy great deeds when neighbor states,/But for thy sword and fortune, trod upon them—' (*Tim.*, IV.iii.93-96).

By similar but still more curious involutions of pride, Coriolanus on two separate occasions denies his inveterate envy of Aufidius and his equal hatred of the people and of the people's representatives. He does so by temporary reflexive, outward pretensions to indifference, as for example, when Coriolanus (then Marcius) first drops the name of Aufidius: 'I sin in envying his nobility;' (I.i.230). In the play's central confrontation between Coriolanus and the Tribunes in III.i, it is insinuated that he is dreadfully disturbed over the people.: 'Choler?... /Were I as patient as the midnight sleep,/By Jove, 'twould be my mind!' (*Cor.*, III.i.84-86).

For her part, when Lady Macbeth bounces onto the stage while Macbeth is about the murder of Duncan, claiming, by rather uneasily proud antitheses, to have been made bold by drink — 'That which hath made them drunk hath made me bold;/What hath quench'd them hath given me fire' (*Mac.*, II.ii.1-2)—it is clear from the terror and fear she evinces immediately after (in her nervous reaction to the

hooting owl and to Macbeth's cry from within) that her bold-
ness involves her unwittingly in horrible paradoxes.

Neither Lady Macbeth nor Coriolanus nor Alcibiades on the
occasions I have quoted can, of course, be said to be guilty
of self-ignorance of the kind demonstrated, for example, by
Cassius or Troilus in earlier citations. The three can all be said
to be aware, in some degree or other, of what they are actually feeling. But they are guilty of self-deception. Just what
representational significance these many forms of duality
possess must be seen to be 'ironic'. They are reflections of a
concern with the problem of self-knowledge that antedates
and postdates the central concern with the problem of a literal representation of passion.

If part of the problem connected with the literal representation of passion lay in the fact that characters could be
too well aware of themselves, so to speak, it could only have
been a pointed irony to Shakespeare that characters could
know themselves too little. In fact, the recognition of self-deception and self-ignorance, no less than the recognition of
tragically helpless emotion (as in the cases of Othello and
Lear above: pp. 45-46), constitutes, in relation to the central
focus on a literal representation of passion, at once ethical
incitement and philosophical brooding.

We have already seen the overt representational significance of excessively and uncontrollably inward emotion in
cases of self-reference in the tragedies (pp. 45-46). The same
significance is implicit in other dramatically contrasting instances. Shakespeare appears to recognize as an obstacle to a
literal representation of passion, on the one hand, *human
inability to sustain* a certain level of intensity of passion, as in
Cleopatra's remark about her fainting reaction to Antony's

death: 'No more but [e'en] a woman, and commanded/By such poor passion as the maid that milks' (*Ant.*, IV.xv.73-74); and, on the other, the herculeanly-sustained experience of emotion so huge as to be unfathomable, as with Gloucester in *King Lear*: 'how stiff is my vild sense/That I stand up, and have ingenious feeling/ Of my huge sorrows!' (IV.vi.279-281).

In instances of self-exposition involving verbal reference to the seat of passion, or of being, the same recognition of the gap possible between outward and inward reality is reflected in some cases again in the form of *self-deception*. A prime example of this is Othello's various pretensions to an untouchable emotional integrity whose tenuousness is spectacularly demonstrated when Othello contemptuously dismisses as preposterous the possibility of ever becoming jealous when, in fact, he is on the verge of the most serious doubts to the effect: 'Exchange me for a goat,/When I shall turn the business of my soul/To such [exsufflicate] and [blown] surmises,/Matching thy inference' (*Oth.*, III.iii.180-183).

It is only somewhat less spectacularly that, at one point, Coriolanus represents his refusal to appease the people in his 'quarrel' with them as a high matter of integrity rather than as the matter of ambiguous pride that it actually is: 'Must I go show them my unbarb'd sconce? Must I/ With my base tongue give to my noble heart/A lie that it must bear? Well, I will do't' (*Cor.*, III.ii.99-101). Integrity is undoubtedly a major and, indeed, a very noble concern of Coriolanus'. But rather than present Coriolanus as a man of positive integrity, most of the action seems clearly designed to express ambiguously, through the continual breakdown of his integrity and the effects on it of the self-deceiving involutions of pride: Coriolanus' *illusion* of it.

The helpless recognition of the unrepresentably inward could not be applied more dramatically than in depicting the elaborate emotional ruses Cleopatra falls to using with Antony. At one point early in the play, after Antony has announced that he is leaving for Rome, Cleopatra counters Antony's disarmingly frank amazement at how far she can go. She makes the claim, clearly designed to confront us with the *paradox*, that her ruses are actually a genuine expression of her inward feeling: ''Tis sweating labor/To bear such idleness so near the heart/As Cleopatra this' (*Ant.*, I.iii.93-95).

One further aspect to the use of self-expository representational techniques remains to be noted. In the preceding pages, I have tried to suggest that in his use of self-expository techniques, Shakespeare shows a motivating concern with the literal representation of passion. Although Shakespeare achieves a partial success with these techniques, he inevitably recognizes their inherent *representational limitations*. This recognition largely takes the form of a contemplation of the inner-outer duality as this is reflected in many uses of the techniques, some of these strikingly dramatic.

Now in other self-expository examples, Shakespeare demonstrates this representational concern and exploration more directly.

5. Tautology

All of the instances that I shall now proceed to cite have in common that they turn upon the inward experience with an intent to represent its essential nature or movement directly. But this representational effort only points out how rather dramatically inadequate is the language especially (since it seems most appropriately) chosen for the purpose.

For instance, in the third scene of the first act of *Othello*, on arriving into the Senate council-chamber, Brabantio stops to justify his failure to address himself to Venice's crisis. He appeals to the indeferably inclusive urgency of his private grief over Desdemona's marriage: 'nor doth the general care/Take hold on me; for my particular grief/Is of so flood-gate and o'erbearing nature/That it engulfs and swallows other sorrows,/*And it is still itself*' (I.iii. 54-58).

To this category of representational technique also belongs the last part of Macbeth's 'Two truths are told' soliloquy, in which Macbeth describes the profoundly non-plussing effects and symptoms of the evil 'suggestion' to murder: 'My thought, whose murther yet is but fantastical/Shakes so my single state of man that function/ Is smother'd in surmise, *and nothing is/ But what is not*' (*Mac.*, I.iii.139-142).

Still another occurence of the device, more difficult to detect principally because of the poetic density of the passage to which it belongs, is to be found in *Antony and Cleopatra*, at the point at which Antony despairs of life and of passion on falsely learning of Cleopatra's 'death': 'for now/All length is torture; since the torch is out,/Lie down and stray no farther. Now all labor/Mars what it does; yea, *very force entangles/Itself* with strength' (IV.xiv. 45-49).

The lines here are difficult and involved, but what Antony is saying is that, because of the inexhaustibly raging strength of his grief, all self-expression would be ineffectual and inadequate. Self-expression would be all the more frustrating because the passion (which would have been strong enough in any circumstances) is made all the stronger and more urgent by Antony's sense of the dishonor and baseness he has incurred by his furious, suspicious hatred of Cleopatra (just before the announcement of her 'death'). The sense of the inadequacy of self-expression is significant, for it reflects the very characteristic sense in *Antony and Cleopatra* of the great futility of self-expression, a futility felt in proportion to the great, changeable complexity of the passions.

Leontes in the heat of his jealousy in *The Winter's Tale* dramatizes similar expressive problems, even if he appears (far more tragically) to have greater facility of insight. He endeavors to trace his emotion to its source: 'Affection! thy intention stabs the centre./Thou dost make possible things not so held,/Communicat'st with dreams (how can this be?),/With what's unreal thou coactive art,/And fellow'st nothing' (I.ii.138-142).

The fact that Leontes' passion is entirely unfounded (while this may at first sight appear to negate the significance of the effort) only makes it more tragically potent. There seems to be a suggestion in the presentation of Leontes' passion that his conviction of Hermione's infidelity is in some sense visionary. He apprehends her faithlessness with the force of a sixth sense: 'Cease, no more./You smell this business with a sense as cold/As is a dead man's nose; but I do see't, and feel't/As you feel doing thus [*grasps his arm*]—and see withal/The instruments that feel' (II.i.150-154).

Although it would be useless to deny that Shakespeare thinks Leontes' passion an absolute error, nevertheless that it is sustained with a seemingly visionary intensity would appear to render it, for that very reason, all the more horribly mysterious. Hence the effort to capture it here despite the absolute irony, paradoxically of the most significant consequence.

In Antony's case, 'very force entangles/Itself with strength' constitutes a special expressive effort, one designed to capture the inward passion elementally, and such an effort is made out of a compelling sense that nothing less could be adequate.

In Macbeth's case especially, 'nothing is but/What is not', one senses the great urgency of the expressive effort. Qualifying Macbeth's effort is a sense that the sphere it addresses might be more properly referred to the divine. But if the unique intensity and incomparable sophistication of Macbeth's effort are any indication, this only seems to have intensified the urgency and seriousness of *the essential problem common to passion and evil alike: the problem of representing inwardness.*

Indeed, all of the instances from this last group without exception dramatize the knowledge or experience of an insight or intuition that it is impossible if imperative to communicate literally. If the terms of this effort are deliberately and appropriately abstract and, perhaps most curiously, tautological — Brabantio's 'And it is still itself'; Macbeth's 'nothing is/But what is not'—the essential impenetrability of these terms only underlines the serious extent of the challenge posed to language by the finally problematic nature of the inward passion.

Part Three

The Coming of Rudolf Steiner and Romantic Evolution

I

Swinburne's view of Othello as 'the noblest man of man's making' exerted in the post-Romantic age the most far-reaching influence.[23] If this is so, it is because in his *Shakespearean Tragedy* A.C. Bradley made of Swinburne's view the standard for an idealization of the Shakespearean hero that does not give sign of having ever given way to another, truer, and more comprehensive vision of Shakespearean tragic production.

Most recently, James Bulman, in *The Heroic Idiom in Shakespearean Tragedy* [24], felt called upon to restate the need for our continued familiarization with that heroic component in the tragic representation which, through our perception of the most horrible failure, generates and continues to sustain our *admiration of the hero* in his absolute dedication to high nobility as he sees it and his noble defiance of his fate. In giving expression to this view once again, Bulman was merely carrying on a very long line of commentary, certainly among *the* most characteristic forms of commentary in this century. The following critics may be seen as constituting our great exponents of the 'heroic' Shakespeare: Howard Baker, Willard Farnham, Moody Prior, Clifford Leech, D.G. James, Peter Alexander, Douglas Bush, Curtis Watson, William Rosen, Eugene Waith, Reuben Brower — the list is almost interminable.[25]

And of course one thinks of Bradley, though from an older tradition, as illustriously spearheading this great line of masterful critics, though no one, as far as I know, has ever remarked upon the overwhelming influence on Bradley of Swinburne and his view of Othello.

Yet the influence of that view may be said to have been responsible for some of the most far-reaching criticism of Shakespeare in this century — not only from Bradley who measured himself against Swinburne, but also from G. Wilson Knight who measured himself in turn against Bradley.

Translating this influence into more modern terms, we might say that in each instance it is the case of the strong critic presuming to have out-wrestled his chief precursor and acknowledged master in heroic criticism.

Thus Bradley perceived in the figure of Othello a form of nobility beyond even Swinburne's inspired ability to perceive:

> This character is so noble, Othello's feelings and actions follow so inevitably from it ... that he stirs, I believe, in most readers a passion of mingled love and pity which they feel for no other hero in Shakespeare..., and to which not even Mr. Swinburne can do more than justice.[26]

The extraordinary significance of Swinburne's influence on Bradley does not become fully apparent until we watch Bradley accomplishing the substitution of Lear for Othello as the figure in whom Shakespeare concentrates his very greatest achievement in high nobility:

> There is nothing more noble and beautiful in literature than Shakespeare's exposition of the effect of suffering in reviving the greatness and eliciting the sweetness of Lear's nature... There is no figure, surely, in the world

of poetry at once so grand, so pathetic, and so beautiful as his… in whom the rage of the storm awakes a power and a poetic grandeur surpassing even Othello's anguish.[27]

How far Swinburne's influence extends cannot be entirely fathomed until we come to G. Wilson Knight and his still more remarkable attempt years later to establish the greater superiority of Timon over both Lear and Othello. Knight could speak now of the unsurpassably 'unswerving majesty' of Timon's passion:

which holds a grandeur beyond the barbaric fury of Othello [limited by the 'barbaric' element], or the faltering ire of Lear [equally limited in being 'faltering'] …it is the recurrent and tormenting hate-theme of Shakespeare developed, raised to an infinite power, …the onrush of a passion which sums in its torrential energy all the lesser passions of those protagonists foregone. Timon is the totality of all, his love more rich and oceanic than all of theirs… he suffers that their pain may cease, and leaves the Shakespearean universe redeemed that Cleopatra may win her Antony in death, and Thaisa be restored to Pericles.[28]

Wilson Knight casts his own great shadow over Shakespearean criticism today. His successful appropriation of the tradition of heroic grandeur to his unrivaled treatment of the abysmal hate-theme in Shakespeare is one which criticism has no knowledge of having ever successfully related to a larger whole or a more comprehensive model of Shakespeare's 'tragic progress'. Thus Timon and his passion may well appear to remain the supreme Shakespearean tragic expression, the very noblest of all: the hero's self-expression in abysmal 'hate' and its truth 'really' represents his nobility and his 'love'.

That maneuver back from 'hate' to 'love' is characteristic. Behind the great tradition of *the heroic criticism of Shakespeare* (behind the criticism of Swinburne, Bradley, Wilson Knight and many others), lies the seemingly irrepressible Romantic and post-Romantic assumption of man's innate grandeur and nobility through what might otherwise appear to us to be the most horribly abysmal and self-damning fate.

Swinburne himself owed his influential view of Othello to what Barbara Everett, writing on *King Lear*, once felicitously described as Romantic sympathy for, or participation in, the central character, involving a view of poetry that is plot-less, 'being, so to speak, rather than becoming'.[29] In this view, all disagreeables in the hero's fate could, and did, ultimately evaporate. And indeed the apotheosis of Lear as hero has the longest history in our post-Romantic age, dating as far back as Lamb:

> while we read it, we see not Lear, but we are Lear—we are in his mind, we are sustained by a grandeur which baffles the malice of daughters and storms...[30]

Part of the special distinction of Everett's essay is that it sought to counter the worst excesses of post-Romantic optimism — which had given us the transcendental, Christian Lear. Everett put forward another standard of Shakespearean heroic grandeur, one which allowed more scope for a more honest acknowledgment of the ironic disagreeables in Shakespeare's representation, on the model of Pascal rather than that of Romanticism:

> though Pascal was a man almost certainly wholly un-
> like Shakespeare in mind, temperament and way of life,
> his writing postulates a world in which it is still possi-
> ble to think both seriously and ironically of *la grandeur
> de l'homme*; and to see that the conditions on which
> such grandeur is based are close to those of tragic
> experience.[31]

But whether Romantic, post-Romantic or Pascalian, the tradition of heroic grandeur lies in the mainstream of Western consciousness. It seems inevitable, then, that, with the perpetuation of that tradition into the twentieth century, there should have been added to it the masterly elucidations of the great twentieth-century scholar-critics who had arrived to prove, beyond trace of a doubt, that the vision of heroic grandeur of their own imagination was one also shared by the Renaissance in which Shakespeare wrote. To the over-whelming certainty of the Romantic imagination of man's innate grandeur, there could now be added the ascertainable authority of the influence on Shakespeare of medieval and classical precedent. The tradition of heroic grandeur ap-peared to have been put beyond the power of any criticism to attribute any other import to Shakespearean tragic repre-sentation.

And yet a criticism of that kind has for some time been in the making in England. Its major value consists precisely in the fact that it has wrestled squarely with the overpowering tradition of heroic criticism. Indeed any criticism which has sought to bypass confronting that tradition has had inevita-bly to suffer judgment on its ineffectuality.

That seems to be the case, for instance, with Helen Gardner's retrospective article on *Othello*[32] in which she ventured to demur against what she recognized as that characteristic 'taste' of twentieth-century Shakespeare criticism for 'a giant art'. In raising to pre-eminence *Lear*, *Macbeth*, and *Timon*, such taste had unfairly relegated *Othello* to an inferior position as a play by comparison disappointingly lacking in grandeur. Gardner claimed that one ought rather to be able to value *Othello* as an extraordinary play in its own right, remarkable for the individuality of its characterization and the concentration of its plot. However, in the face of a tradition of such overpowering significance and authority, Gardner's case really amounted to an admission that *Othello* *is* a lesser play. It would rather have been incumbent on her to show how *Othello* relates to — takes its own distinctive place, as a first breakthrough, in — that unrivaled progress in heroic grandeur which undeniably defines Shakespeare's main achievement in this period.[33]

The paramount significance of the criticism which I shall now proceed to cite is that it successfully related itself to the mainstream of Shakespearean tragic experience. It fully acknowledges all that heroic criticism of Shakespeare had sought to make of that experience. But it brings to light evidence of an embodiment of values in Shakespeare's representation which shows that he does not finally make of heroic grandeur what heroic criticism had us believing. Significantly, the stress of this criticism falls rather on that aspect of the representation which confronts us with all that is *not* in the possession of the hero in his awful pretension to such grandeur.

In *Shakespeare and Tragedy*, John Bayley cites, among many other moments, the 'temple-haunting martlet' speech from

Macbeth (I.vi.3ff) and the goings-on at the foot of Dover Cliff in *Lear* (IV.vi.11ff):

> All... in various ways, disclose kinds of existence out-
> side the preoccupations of their tragic matter... release
> us from the point of view, the preoccupation that, in
> rhetorical form, dominates tragedy... It is a typical
> paradox that Shakespearean tragedy should consist so
> much of angelic moments...which bring home the na-
> ture of the tragic, as his poetry gives it to us, more
> unmistakably than all its rhetoric of loss and darkness,
> misfortune and disaster. The art of Shakespeare draws
> our attention to how free we are from its own material
> and manipulation... gives us a special awareness of
> such freedom; and it seems the same kind of awareness
> that tantalizes the consciousness of Lear and Macbeth,
> Hamlet and Othello. To be aware of it, and yet to be
> deprived of it, is for them the most absolute part of
> tragedy.[34]

The first indications of this strong, *meta-heroic criticism*, if one may so designate it, were in fact first set down firmly by T.B. Tomlinson, in *A Study of Elizabethan and Jacobean Drama*.[35] Here we should turn especially to Tomlinson's opening remarks in his first chapter, 'The Elizabethan Tragic World' (to p.13), and to the chapter 'Shakespearean Trag-edy'.

Tomlinson's treatment of the import of heroic criticism for a later tradition that competes with it remains one of the most central statements. It is perhaps the most significant starting-point for the study of Shakespearean tragedy from this point of view. Its chief value is that it built directly, criti-cally, and fruitfully on the decisive historical contribution to Shakespeare studies of F.R. Leavis, in his *Education and the University*, and L.C. Knights, in *Some Shakespearean Themes*. [36]

For Tomlinson, as for Bayley, the representational indications with the most decisive bearing on Shakespeare's
tragic vision were also to be found in references such as 'the
thick rotundity of the world' in *Lear*: 'We are conscious of
suggestions of vitality springing from the very terms of tragic
protest and tragic destruction'[37]:

> Blow, winds, and crack your cheeks! rage, blow!
> You cataracts and hurricanoes, spout
> Till you have drench'd our steeples,
>   [drown'd] the cocks!
> You sulph'rous and thought-executing fires,
> Vaunt couriers of oak-cleaving thunderbolts,
> Singe my white head! And thou, all-shaking
>   thunder,
> Strike flat the *thick rotundity* o' th' world!
>
> (III.ii.1-7)

In pursuing this line, Tomlinson, faithfully, quotes
F.R. Leavis on the Shakespearean tragic medium:

> For Shakespeare's blank verse is a convention (so sub-
> tle that we forget it to be one) that enables him to play
> upon us, not merely through our sense of the character
> speaking, but also, and at the same time, directly; and
> the question how much of the one and how much of
> the other it may be in any particular case, does not
> arise.

Tomlinson continues:

> The Shakespearean tragic paradox includes... a demon-
> stration that nature, so far from being mere back-
> ground or illustration of a morality or goodness truly
> grounded in man alone [in the face of an alien uni-
> verse] is in itself an indispensable source of nourish-

ment, the given body of experience and substance sustaining and supporting human life. The tragic hero often fails to see this, or sees it only imperfectly. But the plays see it, and consequently see human life as 'closely related to the wider setting of organic growth as indeed, in a quite concrete and practical way, directly based on man's dealings with the earth that nourishes him.' [38]

Whether or not, as a final bearing, this *other* tradition satisfies our sense of Shakespeare's 'tragic progress' better (it opposes itself directly to the tradition of heroic criticism); in what sense, as *an alternative tradition*, it needs itself to be questioned, adjusted, challenged — I want to propose that these are the considerations that should still properly be concerning and absorbing the best efforts in Shakespearean criticism today. For if not, the powerful ghosts of Swinburne, of Bradley and of G. Wilson Knight, to name only the seminal figures in the heroic criticism of Shakespeare, will otherwise pass beyond our chance of ever laying them to rest.

II

The problem we face in dealing with the overpowering tradition of the post-Romantic heroic criticism of Shakespeare is hardly settled by deciding that its great exponents were simply wrong or that we today, with our more learned and more practised forms of criticism, know better. It lies rather with us to strive to recognize and to come to terms with what was, in the hands of these exponents, a very powerful method of knowledge.

That method must be seen as building on that of the Imagination which Owen Barfield, writing in 1944 in *Romanticism Comes of Age*, went so far as to think a momentous advance in the evolution of human consciousness. He found some support for his view at the time in the writings of John Middleton Murry. [39] What Barfield had to say of critics after Schelling and Coleridge, in a re-issue of his book substantially amplified when it came out again in 1966, applies, I believe, to a pre-eminent degree in the case of the great post-Romantic Shakespeareans themselves, that is to say, to Swinburne, Bradley, and Wilson Knight among others:

> Any number of critics following Schelling and Coleridge, have dealt with imagination as an ultimate mental activity that opposes and transmutes into a kind of aesthetic or mystical contemplation that absolute dichotomy between perceiving subject and perceived object on which our practical everyday experience (Coleridge's 'lethargy of custom') is necessarily based. [40]

Shakespearean criticism since the Romantics has, in it most vital and most powerful expressions, been entirely along the lines of the Imagination as set forth by Coleridge in the thirteenth chapter of the *Biographia Literaria*. In Coleridge's terms, 'elevating the thesis' [in our case, Shakespearean tragic experience] came from proceeding *further* 'from [the] notional to [the] actual'. That achievement Coleridge thought specifically made possible by 'contemplating the thesis intuitively ...in the living principle and in the process of our own self-consciousness'. [41] It is unlikely, therefore, that we shall ever come to terms with the full import of Shakespearean criticism since Coleridge without having first penetrated the profound method so memorably captured in these terms.

Contemporary criticism, however, is of course almost brazenly *anti*-Romantic. In practice though especially by profession, it is marked by a contemptuous disbelief that there could ever have been a time when one could say that one believed in nothing so much as the truth of the Imagination. The irony of that predicament is that if our anti-Romantic critics lord it over us today, this is only by the allowance of a profound failure *within Romanticism* itself, a failure which it was Owen Barfield's remarkable achievement to have strenuously uncovered. It was of course Keats who said: 'I am certain of nothing but the holiness of the heart's affections, and the truth of the Imagination.'

'No,' says Barfield:

> Today, we must know in what way the imagination is true. Otherwise we cannot feel its truth.[42]

It was, as Barfield indicates, a matter of grasping 'the true nature of certainty':

> And the first step towards the solution of this problem is the grasping of a right theory of knowledge.[43]

I invoke Barfield's point of view because by no other shall we find our bearings with respect to *the profound impasse into which post-Romantic Shakespearean criticism has fallen* over the course of this century. Because the entire criticism I have cited builds on a method of Imagination in fact *un*elaborated, without that further, certain basis which a right theory of knowledge would have provided, it has for long been easy to dismiss the vision of the hero's grandeur championed centrally by Swinburne, Bradley, Wilson Knight and others, just as it became easy to dismiss Leavis' controverting vision of 'Life':

either you felt Life or you did not. Great literature was
a literature reverently open to Life, and what Life was
could be demonstrated by great literature. The case
was circular, intuitive, and proof against all argument,
reflecting the enclosed coterie of the Leavisites themselves.[44]

Leavis, as we have seen, ushered in a new phase in the
history of Shakespeare criticism in this century. He would
certainly have thought of himself as standing over and against
the Romantic legacy in Shakespeare criticism. But he falls
himself within the pale of its tragedy. It says everything about
the far-reaching influence of Romanticism, and of its tragedy, that Leavis' final formulation of 'the living principle'[45]
should directly echo Coleridge. The phrase is from that very
theory of the Imagination from the *Biographia* to the dramatic *discontinuation* of which Owen Barfield specifically laid
down the tragedy.

The tragedy is one that was mediated by the great post-
Romantic Shakespeareans themselves. Having entered into a
vision of the method of the Imagination, they supposed the
vision *in itself* sufficient and complete, the Imagination 'true'
without feeling the need to pursue the further question 'In
what *way* is Imagination true?'[46]

Post-Romantic Shakespearean criticism today awaits
an account that would make the necessary connections allow-
ing us to relate an original term of *heroic grandeur* (re-discov-
ered for us in such powerful form by our post-Romantic
heroic Shakespeareans) to that opposing term (to which F.R.
Leavis first introduced us) of *a meta-heroic life* established in
direct opposition to the value of the hero.

Between these polar positions (heroic grandeur vs.
meta-heroic life) lies the all-determining area of 'abysmal' fate
into which the hero is plummeted.

The assumption of the complete sufficiency of their vision of the Imagination is what led many of our post-Romantic critics to dwell in the end almost exclusively in its dimension, and to ascribe, *by projection*, a corresponding integrity either to the hero, as in the case of our heroic critics, or, among those of Leavis' following, to Shakespeare himself as poet. What is left unapprehended, by heroic and meta-heroic critics alike, is precisely that 'abysmal' dimension opened up to us by the hero's tragic passion. The final import of this awful 'fall', as a reflection on heroic capacity, has yet to be fully accounted for on the basis of that 'right theory of knowledge' which would include a fully elaborated theory of the Imagination.

Without our penetrating to such an account, there is no likelihood that the post-Romantic heroic criticism of Shakespeare will survive in our estimation as part of a continuous history. But if not, the life of the Shakespeare critic practising today and tomorrow will have become that much the poorer. It will become a haunted life — pursued by the shadow of ghosts who will remain unappeased; though it is still not too late in the day.

III

Rudolf Steiner may be remembered as the man whom Barfield acknowledged to be not only the outstanding influence behind his own work but the great world-historic figure who had come to *supply* what the Romantic Movement itself could not provide.[47] That Steiner was to remain virtually unknown in the literary and academic worlds even to this day is a phenomenon that Barfield could already see developing at the time he was writing. This fact constituted for him the deepest of disappointments. To witness the spectacle of Barfield's frustrated crusade on Steiner's behalf is to see how

Barfield as philosopher-critic — though not as a disciple of Steiner — falls victim himself to the tragedy of the Romantic Movement. But by far the greatest part of the tragedy is that Steiner remains unknown to this day. And at the risk of following in the wake of Barfield's fate as a critic, I myself would wish to insist on the desperate need in our own time to re-affirm the inevitability of Barfield's choice of champion.

To the unanswered problem which the Romantic Movement in literature raised — 'In what way is Imagination true?'— the solution lay in grasping 'a right theory of knowledge'. Barfield has filled out the rest of the story for us:

> Now the Romantic Movement never properly crystallized into a theory of knowledge. In this country — apart from Coleridge — there was hardly even the desire for such a theory. But in Central Europe it was somewhat different. Apart from the group of Romantic philosophers, Goethe, with such conceptions as that of the 'exact percipient fancy' and with all his scientific work, brought an initial confidence in the truth of imagination at any rate to the verge of a theory of knowledge. And Steiner, in his *Philosophy of Freedom*, carried it over that verge and established it firmly in the promised land of philosophy.[48]

If, as Barfield has put it, 'the true *differentia* of imagination is that the subject should be somehow merged or resolved into the object'[49], then, as he points out:

> Only Steiner ...has clearly apprehended this activity as part, and but the first part, of a long, sober process of *cognition* [italics mine] that may end in a man's actually overcoming the dichotomy...[50]

Only in the *continuation of the story*, then — as 'Romanticism comes of age' — do we finally find justification for the supreme value Barfield continued to ascribe in the history of the evolution of consciousness to the activity of Imagination.

In Steiner's case, it was a matter of having to build on 'exact results with the help of a perceptive faculty developed through *controlled* imagination...'[51] From Steiner we learn that the method was one which Goethe had already understood and practised, though he left it undeveloped.[52] The key word here is 'controlled', for the ground-breaking value of Steiner's development of the method is that it is 'in its essence, *systematic imagination*'.[53] As Barfield explains:

> the 'Intuition', in which his method culminates, is to be reached by way of two preliminary stages, the first of which he terms Imagination and the second Inspiration.
>
> It is only at the second of the three stages, that of Inspiration, that the perceptive faculty is enhanced in a way that begins to have objective value *for cognition*[54] [italics mine].

There have been intimations of the 'truth' of the Imagination as early as a hundred years before. But Steiner reveals, in his own comprehensive account of World-evolution, that it develops as the activity of Imaginative *cognition* only in the latter part of the nineteenth century. To associate Rudolf Steiner with a unique phenomenon of the late nineteenth and early twentieth centuries is another way of saying that one cannot approach him separately from the *Anthroposophical* Movement which he not so much founded as mediated.

Here I might add, by way of an autobiographical preliminary, that my own association with this Movement is the result of a combination of events that I should like to think frees me from the necessity of special pleading on behalf of the approach I will be proposing. I came to the Anthroposophical Movement along two routes — at once from the side of Anthroposophy *and* of Literature. My membership in this Movement is primarily, of course, my own choice of life, but it is also, partly and crucially, the eventual result of the influence of personal associations in my life who were themselves associated with the Movement from an early age (for Anthroposophy — about twenty-eight; I speak of a full intellectual association, for Anthroposophical *culture*, of course, extends to every phase of life, as witnessed in the Waldorf schools founded on the basis of its principles.)

Anthroposophy was in my life long before I myself found a personal relation to it. In the meantime, my research (for my doctoral dissertation) into the relationship between metaphorical language and an otherworldly reality led me by a natural course of discovery, and along an entirely independent route, to Owen Barfield's *Poetic Diction*.

In a later edition of this work, Barfield formally acknowledges his debt to Rudolf Steiner. Barfield's association with Anthroposophy was, until then, unknown to me. And as I came to him then, so I come to him again now, though conscious now of a relation that I bear myself to Rudolf Steiner from my own place within the Anthroposophical Movement.

The task facing a Shakespeare critic who is also an Anthroposophist is beset with the greatest difficulty. The history of the Anthroposophical Movement itself testifies to the tragedy of misguided attempts to apply the results of Anthroposophical research directly to non-Anthroposophical areas of life.

Anthroposophy became drastically changed in the process: to see the tragedy from the other side.

But the obverse may also be true — namely, that it is impossible to approach the concepts which Anthroposophy yields without finally making the leap into Anthroposophy itself. What this means is that a Shakespeare critic who is also an Anthroposophist will always be conscious that his concepts are derived from within another experience: the *first-hand* experience of Anthroposophy.

With Rudolf Steiner, the idea of the 'wisdom of man', or *Anthropo-Sophia*, is suddenly greatly extended. It is accompanied by a fully developed account of how, 'in the process of our own self-consciousness', we work our way cognitively into the World-process, in Imagination, Inspiration and Intuition.

Concepts are yielded which even critics who are not Anthroposophists will acknowledge fit the case of Shakespeare in a way that will appear inevitable. This is a direct consequence of the astonishing comprehensiveness of the vision of World-evolution Steiner acquired on the basis of the higher cognitive powers.

Nowhere, for instance, but in Steiner shall we find a fully developed account of that tremendous otherworldly experience from which modern man has become tragically alienated, bearing out the view that 'from the fifteenth century onwards humanity has been gradually forsaken by the Gods'.[55] My own record of that process of alienation as presented in my book, *Otherworldly Hamlet,* written independently of Anthroposophy, by comparison has the value of a distant intuition, though it would appear that I *was* feeling my way in the right direction.[56] Just how far the process of alienation was meant to go for Shakespeare, or why it had to go that far, likewise cannot be grasped without the benefit of Anthroposophy. This is the view I will be highlighting in this chapter.

I know of no account that does more justice to the comprehensive nature of Shakespeare's progressive experience in tragedy than the account of *what Anthroposophy calls the 'Consciousness Soul'-experience* put forward by Barfield himself with special reference to Shakespeare as its most representative instance:

> Seek death! Yes, *know* yourself and the world! Do not merely *believe* in the old way, substituting one creed for another. Rather live in the breakdown of all belief. Even encourage your own opposition, as men do in games. Immerse in the destructive element! And so learn to tear your true self free from all thought and all feeling in which the senses echo.[57]

Experience cannot be pure, or complete, unless a renunciation has first been made.

A life of thought and feeling given over to the world of the senses Steiner saw as the characteristic experience of the *Sentient Soul*. Where thought and feeling combine in the act of faith, we have the characteristic experience of the *Intellectual or Mind Soul*. The experience of the *Consciousness Soul* — of the self alone — falls in between these two Soul-experiences, in absolute separation from them both.

The world of Shakespeare's tragedies marks the point where the Consciousness Soul-experience is brought to bear on inherited forms of faith and of sensual engagement that, for reasons that cannot be grasped at that time, have now to be renounced. The renunciation itself is a profoundly tragic experience. A perversely hopeful notion continues to be entertained at this time as to what it is that can be had in the way of 'faith' or a 'life of the senses'.[58]

Characteristically, a great power of 'faith' is being brought to bear on an experience of 'love' in sensual terms. And that is precisely what has become *unreal* as experience. An element of absolute freedom from these terms must first be introduced, before a right relation to them can be restored.

It is precisely Shakespeare's great achievement at this time that *he* unconsciously supplies the mediating role. He embodies in himself the standard of true consciousness by which the attitudes of his characters, in respect of faith and of love, are judged wanting. Shakespeare's own role in this regard is far from being an indifferent one, as indicated in Barfield's point that he was 'only unconsciously the bearer of — consciousness'.[59] It is as if Shakespeare could not himself accept the profound failure implied in the self's tragic dissociation from any sure basis in faith and in love.

The extent of his identification with the situations of his characters is reflected dramatically in that characteristic impulse to provide a complete representation for his characters in their aims, even where these aims have become perverse. The attempt itself may appear to us perverse, though to see it that way would be wrongly to dissociate ourselves from the profound evolution in experience Shakespeare was himself living through at the time, if only as creative genius.

One main line of development in Shakespeare's 'tragic progress' traces the route that would have to be taken, if an experience of faith and of love were pursued without regard to the further evolution now necessitated. Wilson Knight's comprehensive tracing of the abysmal hate-theme in Shakespeare's tragedies remains, from this point of view, of tremendous critical value.[60]

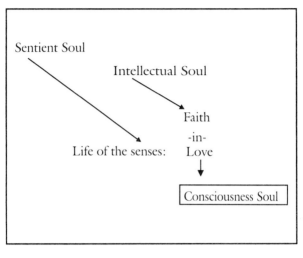

'Hate' is the name Knight gave to an extreme form of violent cynicism about 'love' that overtakes many of Shakespeare's heroes from the time their own deepest aspirations regarding love are confounded. They themselves are thrown into utter confusion. But that such 'hate' in the last analysis denotes the final *negation* of love in *all* the forms Shakespeare's characters present love to us — here is a further view that no critic has been ready to embrace, it would appear in the absence of concepts that would account for such radical developments.

Knight's own approach to Hamlet is a case in point. Knight acknowledges that what now absorbs Hamlet as experience implies not less than 'the negation of any passion whatsoever'.[61] Hamlet, Knight tells us, 'has seen through the tinsel of life and love'. Hamlet is 'right' —his 'philosophy' is 'inevitable, blameless, and irrefutable'.[62] But, in spite of

Knight's acknowledgment that this is true, we find him strangely backtracking, appealing finally to the 'intuitive faith, or love, or purpose, by which we must live if we are to remain sane'.[63] And so, on the basis of this view, Knight finally rejects Hamlet's experience, for 'it is the negation of life. It is death.'[64]

Yet, as we have seen — 'Seek death!'; 'Immerse in the destructive element!' — these are the great *dicta* of the Consciousness Soul-experience, though they are to be known *in Imagination only*, as Barfield's account implies. Hamlet we must see merely as the vehicle for Shakespeare's own evolution in consciousness. There can be no question, consequently, of a direct application of Hamlet's attitudes to life. This is part of the confusion that will be found to underlie Knight's view (notwithstanding his championing of a new form of 'imaginative' criticism at the time he wrote).

That one can embrace a concept of destruction and death without this bearing at all outwardly in the circumstances of life is a crucial consideration that would appear to be beyond the understanding of a certain kind of criticism. However, it explains why Shakespeare himself could entertain such violent concepts in his plays with no corresponding manifestation to show in the outer circumstances of his own life (unlike in the case of Marlowe).

Any confusion between the sphere of the Imagination and the sphere of Life understandably concerns criticism, and such concern reflects on what would appear to be a very real risk involved in entertaining such concepts. The danger is amply illustrated, for example, in the horrid self-indulgence that accompanies Martin Luther's exhortations to the people of his day to know themselves better as sinners. [65]

Luther's *desiderata* had, astonishingly, been taken literally as attitudes to be embodied in life, and Luther was, of
course, horrified. He knew only too well that such knowledge was to be had strictly as an experience of the soul. But
perhaps because the act of Imagination would have to bear
fruit as a real or *objective* process in the soul, Luther may be
said to have been himself guilty of soiling the waters? At any
rate, from the tone of his approach, it is easy to see how his
auditors would have been misled:

> Come, accept. Be a sinner! *Esto peccator!* And don't do
> the thing by halves; sin squarely and with gusto, *pecca
> fortiter!* Not just playful sins. No, but real, substantial,
> tremendous sins![66]

Luther himself may have been guilty of excess in his
approach to it, but the process of Imagination he espouses is
the same. 'Seek death': Luther's is, also, an account of the
Consciousness Soul-experience, though he gives it to us *un*-
consciously, inasmuch as the experience is still being expressed in traditional terms, as a concept of 'sin'. Yet Luther
was also capable of an approach to the experience in non-tra-
ditional terms, as evidenced in his remarkable statement that
'nothing can cure libido'. And in spite of Shakespeare's own
adoption of the traditional language of devilry, sin and so on,
his own approach is initially through a concept of 'lust' (in
Hamlet). Primarily, it is a concept of 'evil' (evident from
Hamlet onwards) and especially a concept of the overpowering *violence* of evil.[67] Before the power of that violence and the hero's conception of that violence, all
faith in love would wither.

It is not difficult to see what horrible uncertainty must
attend on such an experience. Being primarily given to such
faith, the Shakespearean hero is very far from ready for the
experience. And where such faith most clearly takes on heroic

proportions — from *Othello* onwards, where full expression in the 'Intellectual or Mind Soul' continues in the old way—the bewilderment and disillusion would have to be very great. The spectacle of the hero's tragic fall into abysmal hatred becomes an awful one to behold.[68]

The great service performed by our post-Romantic heroic critics of Shakespeare lies in the attempt to re-discover and preserve a proper sense of the full grandeur and scope of the Shakespearean tragic spectacle. Lacking the insight and vision of Anthroposophy, however, they were finally without the conception of a further evolutionary relation to evil implied in Shakespeare's own creative relationship to this material. That they would not have derived that conception for themselves can be deduced from the nature of the material .

The spectacle of evil in Shakespeare's tragedies is so very sinister and finally so overpoweringly violent, it is easy to see why these critics would have reverted to the original spirit of heroic faith for an establishing of 'values'. For them, 'morality or goodness [is] truly grounded in man alone [in the face of an alien universe]'.

It is true that the evil finally overpowers the hero from without. Though it works into him inwardly, the hero himself is tragically helpless before that evil. *The evil is*, that is to say, *elusively and uncontrollably inward*; and this would appear finally to exonerate the hero. So that it is easy to see how in a certain case identification with the hero would continue.

But this is finally to overlook the hero's own radical implication in this evil — among other things, his own abysmal fall into hatred, from which he never fully recovers. Thus, Hamlet might say:

Othello's Sacrifice

If Hamlet from himself be ta'en away,
[...]
Then Hamlet does it not, Hamlet denies it

(V.ii.234ff),

likewise Othello:

That's he that was Othello; here I am.

(V.ii.284)

Shakespeare's heroes in this way dissociate themselves from what has tragically taken place. But, by then, Ophelia and Desdemona, both, lie dead. One thinks also of Cordelia dead in Lear's arms. And in all these cases, the hero's fall into hatred has very substantially contributed to the deaths.

The spectacle of evil in Shakespeare finally transmutes itself into the spectacle of violent death *via* the hero's hatred, itself the involuntary and bitter negation of faith in love. That hatred is also by implication — in the violence of its effect — *negation of the heroic*. In fact, any view which continues to espouse the nobility of the hero in the face of the spectacle of evil Shakespeare offers us must eventually founder against the final emphasis on the violent death of a loved one, for which the hero has become (in a sense that is new in terms of the heroic) hopelessly responsible.

No idea of expression in heroic spirit can be finally reconciled to that aspect of the spectacle. Before these deaths Shakespeare's heroes stand, whether consciously or unconsciously, at an absolute loss. They are, moreover, in a substantial sense that is pointless to deny, guilty of them. Nor can they make amends. On the other hand, it is no more possible to reserve from this aspect of the spectacle the idea of some greater Life that remains intact from the debâcle. Here also it is the case of a tradition of critics who found themselves either indisposed or unable to allow for the value of a spectacle so overwhelmingly violent. To that other idealization of 'nature' (as 'the given body of experience and substance sustaining and supporting human life'), we may oppose the following emphasis from the ending of *King Lear*:

> I know when one is dead, and when one lives;
> She's dead as earth.
>
> (V.iii.261-262)

> No, no, no life
> Why should a dog, a horse, a rat, have life,
> And thou no breath at all? Thou'lt come no more,
> Never, never, never, never, never.
>
> (V.iii.306-309)

That Shakespeare through his verse works directly on us, as Leavis insisted, to suggest other experiences that are possible beyond the immediate tragic spectacle we are being offered, will be readily admitted. It is on this basis that Bayley himself makes a point of the fact that 'the art of Shakespeare draws our attention to how free we are from its own material and manipulation... gives us a special awareness of such freedom'. But this is to say no more but that the process of Life continued for Shakespeare *alongside* the process of tragic representation that absorbed him as creative genius.

By the time we get to the ending of *King Lear*, the process of '*Life' itself* is being *re-valued*, in the face of a more absorbing concern with the all-levelling power that evil could have in Shakespeare's Imagination. We may suppose that what added to the difficulty of seeing just where the spectacle of evil might lead is the fact that Shakespeare does not appear to have himself known what value there could be to the spectacle, except that submission to it appeared to him to be the truest experience in consciousness. In Anthroposophy, one would say that it is *in the nature of* the Consciousness Soul-experience that one cannot know or understand.

The overriding focus which I am saying finally crystal-lizes the essence of Shakespearean tragedy for us is not brought to complete expression until the ending of *King Lear*. It is already, however, anticipated in the ending of *Othello*, which suggests that Shakespeare was working his way progressively *towards* that later point. Othello, unlike Lear, cannot find words to express it, but his own fate comes round to the same obsessive focus:

> O Desdemon! dead, Desdemon! dead!
> O, O!

(V.ii.281-282)

In spite of the sublime expression in romantic-transcendental faith we are given at the beginning of this scene, there is no altering the course events are taking. In the end, Othello simply does not get Desdemona back, though Shakespeare continues to tempt us in our hopes that Desdemona may yet escape death, as she recovers breath twice in this scene, speaking on one occasion:

> Othello: Not dead? not yet quite dead?

(V.ii.86)

> Emilia: O, who hath done this deed?
> Desdemona: Nobody; I myself.
>
> (V.ii.123-124)

Ever since Johnson first declared the ending of *King Lear* itself a scene not to be 'endured', echoing with this comment his similar comment on the ending of *Othello*, critics have striven, in every manner and form, to circumvent the impression of all-levelling hopelessness on which the later scene especially appears to insist.[69] Only Nicholas Brooke in our time has sought strenuously to keep us to the way Shakespeare insists on our seeing it:

> We are driven to see, not only the very human pain of Lear's end with Cordelia in his arms, but also the absolute negation of all forms of hope...
>
> Her death kills all life.[70]

There is no getting around, or away from, the ending of *King Lear*. Shakespeare may have had to continue to trace the course of the hero's hatred through, as Wilson Knight proposed, if only to ensure that the hatred would be finally purged. He would have had to take us, that is to say, as far as *Timon of Athens*, taking up again a play he had already commenced. And along with *Timon*, he would have also had to give us *Antony and Cleopatra* and *Coriolanus*, simply because an attachment to heroic faith would not die so easily.

This is apart from the fact that Shakespeare, as a member of his age, was more or less bound to continue working in the 'heroic idiom', at least for a time longer.[71] It would take much to break the illusion of the value of heroic spirit. It may be that it is never really and finally broken even in

Shakespeare, as far as the outward evidence will say. But certainly with the ending of *King Lear, there is no further way to go*. Either there *is* no hope, as the ending suggests, and we *are* deluded about the surviving value of love, faith and all systems of life in the familiar forms we know — we are deluded, also, about the value of the heroic — or it may be that there is a further purpose to an enforced renunciation of these forms.

Brooke himself could offer no notion of any further purpose to Shakespeare's final focus as given to us in that ending. Such a focus might well appear to us pointless. But here again it is Steiner who, speaking out of the Anthroposophical Movement, provides the necessary vision:

> At this point a possibility comes in which may prove terrible. A man may lose his sensations and feelings of outer reality without finding a new reality opening up before him. He then feels himself as if suspended in the void. He feels bereft of all life. The old values are gone and no new ones have arisen in their place. The world and man no longer exist for him. Now, this is by no means a mere possibility. It happens at one time or another to everyone who seeks higher knowledge. He comes to a point at which the spirit represents all life to him as death...

> We understand this when we know from experience the point of transition from lower to higher knowledge. We ourselves had felt as if all solid matter and things of sense had dissolved into water, and as if the ground were cut away from under our feet. Everything which we had previously felt to be alive had been killed. The spirit had passed through the life of the senses like a sword piercing a warm body, we had seen the blood of sensuality flow. [72]

At a certain point we shall be unable to follow Shakespeare any further in his progress in tragic vision without referring ourselves to an account of the path to higher knowledge, along the lines of the one Steiner himself provided as the path appropriate for our own time. Insofar as we approach this 'path' from the side of Literature — embracing Shakespeare's experience as reflected to us in the literature he left us — it is a question of seeing that no study of the tragedies can be really thorough which does not finally set them in direct relation to the higher processes of the later romances.

The renunciation of all systems of life to which the tragedies bear such tremendous witness as a whole has its justification, finally, only in the higher 'life' that emerges from that renunciation, corresponding to the experience as given in the romances. An idea of 'tragic progress', in this context, necessarily presupposes a further evolutionary relation to a triumphing evil, even in the overwhelmingly final form we get in the ending of *King Lear*. The key lies in the transition from *King Lear* to *Pericles*. Crucial to our understanding of this transition is an implied shift in focus away from the experience of the tragic hero to the transfigured mind of Shakespeare himself.

A new life has already appeared. And the process by which it has come about is now to be outlined for us in a new form of 'allegorical' representation richly suggestive of the experience that lies behind, that is Shakespeare's own.

The distinguishing characteristic of Shakespeare's representation in the tragedies may be said to lie in his progressive
accentuation of the literal status of the tragedy, culminating
in the ending of *King Lear*. It would be grossly to miscon-
ceive of the very different approach taken to the representation of action in *Pericles* to suppose that the characters
of Thaisa or Pericles, or Marina, or the tragedy that befalls
them, are invested with anything like the same literal status.

We have, with *Pericles*, moved far beyond an art which
holds the mirror up to nature, where evil and death literally
prevail. We are on firm ground with the action of *Pericles*
when we see it rather as mirroring allegorically what evil and
death have finally made and are making of themselves in
Shakespeare's own mind. This would seem to be already evident from the obituary Pericles pronounces over Thaisa who
is dead before we have known her:

> Most wretched queen!
> [...] A terrible child-bed hast thou had, my dear,
> No light, no fire. Th' unfriendly elements
> Forgot thee utterly, nor have I time
> To give thee hallow'd to thy grave, but straight
> Must cast thee, scarcely coffin'd, in [the ooze],
> Where, for a monument upon thy bones,
> The [e'er]-remaining lamps, the belching whale,
> And humming water must o'erwhelm thy corpse,
> Lying with simple shells.
>
> (III.i.54-64)

'Lying with simple shells' reflects back to us a kind of
assimilation of a loved one's death inconceivable to one who
has just been through the tragedy. Already, we are alerted to
the fact that Pericles cannot be viewed as a character who is

literally undergoing tragedy here, any more than we have a conception of Thaisa herself as a character.

I do not want to deny, on the other hand, that a literal death has taken place — quite the contrary. It is precisely what makes the 'allegorical' form of representation in which Shakespeare had now chosen to work so amenable to his purpose that a death has certainly occurred, and it is irreversible. We are on firm ground with Pericles' speech, however, only when we see it as representing the effect which the death of a loved one has had over time. The death percolates down, as it were, to the bottom of the mind (represented here as the sea-floor) to become *there* the simple event it could never have been when it actually happened. It is from such point *in* the mind — Shakespeare's own — that Thaisa is then 'returned' from death, by no means as a literal personage.

Approached in this way, Pericles is nothing in himself. He is everything when seen as echoing in himself the Shakespearean tragic hero's experience as this continues to reverberate in Shakespeare's own mind in the extreme and final form to which it had come. Addressing himself to the death that has occurred, Pericles remarks of his loved one, with a truth that fits the case literally: 'Th'unfriendly elements/Forgot thee *utterly*.' Earlier he had said: 'I do not fear the flaw,/It hath done to me the *worst*' (III.i.39-40). Awareness of the extremity of the evil undergone is also reflected in the words Pericles pronounces over the 'child' that is born with, and of, destruction and death:

> a more blusterous birth had never babe.
> [...]Thou art the rudeliest welcome to this world
> That ever was prince's child.

> (III.i.28;31-32)

Othello's Sacrifice

Focus is *on the death that ends all life*, and all corresponding attachments to life. It cannot, therefore, appear how any new or ongoing life can contain anything within itself to compensate for the destruction:

> Even at the first
> Thy loss is more than can thy portage quit.
>
> (III.i.34-35)

And yet, already a new life has appeared, though Pericles does not himself as yet bear any consciousness of this.

That he does *not* testifies to the lingering power of the tragic experience in Shakespeare's mind, though the circumstances in which Pericles finds himself already imply an evolution out of that experience.

From this point, it no longer suffices to think in terms of an experience in the Consciousness Soul alone, which we have as a universal possession in our own day. We have the experience, and yet, if the course Shakespeare took in his tragedies is any indication, we seem unable to follow the full process of that experience through.

We live, for the most part today, *in* the Consciousness Soul. We are otherwise happily or not so happily related in what are, in fact, remnants of the Sentient Soul and Intellectual or Mind Soul experiences; while more and more in critical trends today — by which I mean post-structuralist, postmodern, anti-Romantic— the pretension is to make a principle of the Consciousness Soul alone, as if there never were or could be any other Soul-experiences.

And so do critics today deny in their criticism (and to their students) what they themselves could never do without in their own lives, even as remnants. For the Consciousness Soul-experience has no meaning alone —in itself it is death — and the superior value of the critics I have enumerated who were working in the shadow of Romantic tradition lies precisely in their (at least unconscious) admission of other Soul-experiences that are possible, where meaning actually resides.

From Anthroposophy we learn that it was in the 'Egypto-Chaldean Age' (around 2800-700 B.C.) that the Sentient Soul received its full development; in the 'Graeco-Roman Age' (700 B.C.-1400 A.D.) that the Intellectual or Mind Soul received development. The Consciousness Soul is in process of being developed today, and will continue to develop, the 'Consciousness Soul Age' extending from approximately 1400 A.D. to 3500 A.D.. The 'Imaginative Soul', as the first fruit of the Consciousness Soul-experience, emerges around the beginning of the nineteenth century. A further development in Imagination, Inspiration, and Intuition takes place with Steiner in the late nineteenth and early twentieth centuries. All three additional Soul powers will not, however, become the common possession of whole groups of humanity until much later on, in Ages to come; and we are meant to see each new Soul faculty as emerging in turn out of the others.

Barfield, in *Romanticism*, describes the entire evolution as follows:

> We may very well compare the self of man to a seed. Formerly, what is now seed was a member of the whole plant, and, as such, was wholly informed with a life not wholly its own. But now the pod or capsule has split open, and the dry seed has been ejected. It has attained

to a separate existence. Henceforth one of two things may happen to it: either it may abide alone, isolated from the rest of the earth, growing dryer and dryer, until it withers up altogether; or, by uniting with the earth, it may blossom into a fresh life of its own. Thus it is with the Consciousness Soul. Either it may lose itself in the arid subtleties of a logistic intellectualism, which no longer has any life, though it once had — preoccupying itself with a nice balancing and pruning of dogma, theory and memory — or, by uniting itself with the Spirit of the Earth, with the Word, it may blossom into the Imaginative Soul, and live...

It will be easiest to plunge *in medias res* and to inquire precisely what Steiner said of the further development of the human Ego beyond this stage of the consciousness soul. We have arrived, then, at the point of development at which the macrocosm is so to speak focused to an invisible point in the isolated Ego. What next? The answer of anthroposophy is that there are two alternatives open to it: ultimate death or nonentity on the one hand, and on the other the first step towards an expansion outward again to the macrocosm — an expansion of such nature that the centre and source of life is henceforward within instead of without...

Let us, for the moment, express the whole course of human evolution in the following diagram:

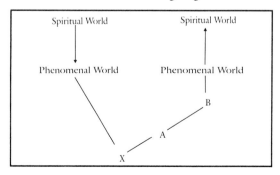

Then, if the point A is the consciousness soul, B represents the developed consciousness soul, the consciousness soul on its way to becoming what Dr. Steiner once called the 'Imaginative Soul'. And at X, which marks the intellectual soul, we have, says anthroposophy, the human nadir, the true mystery of the resurrection, the mystery of the New Man from the Old. Let us look at it historically:

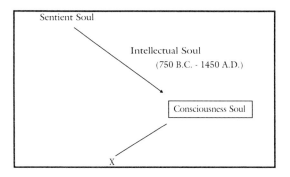

The result is that one begins to assert with confidence, and out of one's own experience, that some remarkable event must have taken place at X, some gift of power to arise from the depths, some passing over of life and meaning from the macrocosm to the microcosm, some mystery, let us say, of resurrection.[73]

Unable to see their way through to the evolutionary relation among these experiences, Romantic and post-Romantic critics were unable to see precisely how the process of meaning is established. These critics could not see how at their best they themselves were profiting from a heightened form of consciousness that was the direct result of this process of meaning being established *as historical process*.

Here is another of those tremendous insights that Anthroposophy has to offer. It would appear that Shakespeare was someone who went through this historical process directly.

Born as the first fruit of the process of the Consciousness Soul-experience is what, in one form of denomination, *Anthroposophy calls the 'Imaginative Soul'*. This is, in its first full-fledged, historical manifestation, none other than what Coleridge and other Romantics would identify as the 'Imagination' — that new, expansive Soul-power proceeding from and in 'the process of self-consciousness' which, for Middleton Murry, also represented a fundamental evolution in human consciousness. Romantic, as well as post-Romantic, critics were thus among the first to be aware of this new Soul-power, in their approach to Shakespeare as in other matters.

But the Imaginative Soul does not, in fact, fully *objectify* itself in Shakespeare until well *after* the process of the Consciousness Soul-experience has run its course.

It is from this point that Romantic and post-Romantic critics alike, operating without the benefit of Anthroposophy, neglected to understand how the full process of the Imagination sees itself through.

They were not able to see that a fully effective Imagination stands in an essential and continuous relationship *with* the Consciousness-Soul experience.

From the side of Literature, we may say that *a first objectification of the Imaginative Soul in Shakespeare* coincides with his presentation of the birth of Marina. But not until Marina's 'coming of age', and Pericles' later 'recognition' of her, is the vision of this Soul power first brought to fully conscious expression. Anthroposophy speaks of the Imaginative Soul in association also with the Spirit Self or Higher Ego. This last term reminds us that the evolution in question emerges fundamentally as a further development of Ego-consciousness. In the structure of this evolution, Marina objectifies that new, *higher* power in the Ego, expressing itself *in* the Imaginative Soul. This power is then shown slowly lifting the Ego in its suffering aspect, represented by Pericles, out of its experience of death in the Consciousness Soul.

We come by this route, then, to one of the most sublime moments in Shakespeare — the so-called recognition-scene between Pericles and Marina. At this stage of the 'progress', the suffering Ego has recognized, and is uniting with, a higher aspect in itself which, though perfectly sensitive to suffering, is yet insusceptible to despair. Pericles himself notes of Marina:

> Yet thou dost look
> Like Patience gazing on kings' graves, and smiling
> Extremity out of act.
>
> (V.i.137-139)

What union with a higher power of Ego now opens up is, in fact, the prospect of a new 'life' in which *the Ego* can be fully *reconciled to tragedy*. Shakespeare's symbol of an extreme, destructive evil (the sea) converts in this context into the symbol of new joy:

> Pericles: O Helicanus, strike me honored sir,
> Give me a gash, put me to present pain,
> Lest this great *sea* of joys rushing upon me

O'erbear the shores of my mortality,
And drown me with their sweetness
[*to Marina*]
                    O, come hither,
Thou that beget'st him that did thee beget...

                                        (V.i.190-195)

Opening out on the vision of Diana (V.i.240ff), new joy now leads Pericles back to Thaisa who is herself an other-than-literal personage. She is not the loved one who has been lost to death, but, rather, all that was lost as a consequence of that death: a 'lost connection to the world' following on 'lost faith' in *all* systems of life. That connection and that faith are what are now restored to the Ego, the consequence of acts of preservation as well as of guidane (as in the case of the vision of Diana) that open out on still other mysteries that concerned Shakespeare at this time. For the allegorical implications of the action in Shakespeare's romances are extensive, indeed vast.

However, the Ego's *restoration to the world*, in faith and in love as well as to the senses, represents, at this stage, an altogether different experience from what connection to the world was before. The whole experience takes place now on a higher plane. Shakespeare's experience in this regard is only partially reflected to us in that additional, ethereal Soul-quality in the verse which every commentator on the romances recognizes is new and is first sighted in this play (though its significance has never before been defined in terms of a consistent theory of meaning). We understand Shakespeare's experience primarily through an allegorical structure that Shakespeare has built into the qualitative representation, from which we gather the greater development or progress that now engages him far beyond the confines of this (or any other) single play.

The development or progress in question extends over both *Pericles* and *The Winter's Tale*. We find the same fundamental experience at the basis of the action in the later play, with Leontes substituting for Pericles, Perdita for Marina, and Hermione for Thaisa. But with this new addition: that the whole is approached, in this instance, from the point of view of the Ego's guilt or direct responsibility for tragedy.

Thus *Pericles* gives us the experience from the point of view of the Ego's innocence in tragedy, *The Winter's Tale* from the point of view of the Ego's guilt. And only in the combined effect of *both* plays, as the expression of what is taking place in Shakespeare's own mind, do we find the evolution that corresponds fully to the experience of Shakespeare's tragic hero who is himself, of course, both innocent *and* guilty.

In light of what has been said thus far, we will not be surprised to find *The Tempest* extending representation of the fundamental experience still further. Here, however, we have a momentous 'return' to the literal level and well-rounded characterization of the tragedies, reflected in a dramatic foregrounding of the principal characters, Prospero and Miranda.

Here, again, there is the case of a loved 'wife' who is lost to death, coinciding with the birth of a 'daughter'. Miranda, we are told, is 'not/Out three years old' (I.ii.40-41), when she and Prospero are put out to sea. The mother is, thus, only recently dead, and not so long before that we cannot see her death as coinciding with Prospero's renunciation of state and devotion to study, or, for that matter, with Mi-

randa's birth. The whole action is an integrated one.
Prospero's decision to 'neglect' all 'worldly ends, all dedi-
cated/To closeness and the bettering of my mind' may be
directly referred to Shakespeare's own evolution, since the
'death' of a loved one became, for him, his one, essential
tragic preoccupation.

Prospero incurs further consequences for his 'decision'
being, along with Miranda, ambushed and driven out to 'sea'
in what presents itself as yet another marvelous transfigura-
tion of the essential tragic sorrow:

> There they hoist us,
> To cry to th' *sea*, that roar'd to us; to sigh
> To th' winds, whose pity, sighing back again,
> Did us but loving wrong.
> Mir.   Alack, what trouble
> Was I then to you!
> Pros.   O, a cherubin
> Thou wast that did preserve me. Thou didst smile,
> Infused with a fortitude from heaven,
> *When I have deck'd the sea with drops full salt,*
> Under my burthen groan'd, which rais'd in me
> An undergoing stomach, to bear up
> Against what should ensue.

> (I.ii.148-158)

It is the 'whole' sorrow that comes to expression once
again here, the death of a loved one being at the center of it.
The supporting power is, likewise, bestowed by Miranda as
higher power, according to the pattern already described. We
may take it as an implicit understanding that the whole evolution Shakespeare has reflected to us in the romances is here
climactically embodied — insofar as literature can embody
this — in Prospero and Miranda as literal inheritors of that

evolution. That we have 'returned' to the literal level in this play will also explain, among other things, why in this instance Prospero's 'wife' is *not* restored, for there can be no question of restoration at this level.

Other variations on the fundamental experience that underlies these plays may be observed, notably the fact that in *The Winter's Tale* the loved one is 'kept' alive. I would suggest that this latest representational gambit was conceived with the intention of intensifying comparison between the order or level of representation as given in the end of the play and our imagination of what a literal restoration of the loved one might be like.

But the comparison works in a way opposite to what we might think. The purpose, it would appear, is to suggest that the experience of being restored to the world has *the same value as* a literal restoration of the loved one, though it may even be that we are being directed to speculate on some further meeting with the loved one after death. The Hermione who speaks at the end, in any case, speaks in the tones of one who is dead, like a revenant. Certainly the idea that the loved one would have kept alive and silent over sixteen years cannot be literally credited, puts far too great a strain on credibility in literal terms. In fact, it would appear that Shakespeare arbitrarily kept Hermione alive, in order to get us to speculate on a whole number of effects other than a literal restoration of the loved one.

With each new play, a new element or aspect of Shakespeare's experience is revealed. Concentration in *Pericles* lies with the emergence and recognition of a higher power of Ego (Marina) expressing itself freely in the Imagination beyond tragedy. On the plane of innocence, a higher power of

Ego is clearly in itself sufficient to lift the Ego out of tragedy. Hence, that peculiar limitation to the quality of the representation in *Pericles*, as if the whole drama were taking place inside the Mind, with no further substantial connection to Nature.

The case is different with *The Winter's Tale*. Here the greater problem of the Ego's guilt is addressed, the different concern corresponding to a significant extension of focus beyond the Ego *into* the realm of Nature. In keeping with the evolution I have been tracing, the saving power in this instance depends crucially on a relation to Nature established in the higher Ego (through Perdita). Concentration here, however, is not on the higher Ego itself so much as on a still greater ordering Power in Nature outside the Ego which the higher Ego yet mediates.

Beyond an experience in the Consciousness Soul, Anthroposophy also speaks of an experience of Imagination, of Inspiration and of Intuition, with one experience leading into the other. Conforming with that evolution, we notice, with new developments in *The Winter's Tale*, a corresponding *extension of the operation of the Imaginative Soul* to a point inside 'great creating Nature' (IV.iv.88) where a great Inspirational order is now revealed. Here we reach the realm of *systematic* Imagination — of regenerative, evolutionary creation —where a higher life is constantly being re-created out of death. It is Perdita who expresses this (it is Florizel who signals her value to us in these terms):

> What you do
> *Still betters* what is done. When you speak, sweet,
> I'ld have you do it ever; when you sing,
> I'ld have you buy and sell so; so give alms;
> Pray so; and for the ord'ring your affairs,
> To sing them too. When you dance, I wish you

100

> A wave o' th' sea, that you might ever do
> Nothing but that; *move still, still so* —
> And own no other function. Each your doing
> (So singular in each particular)
> Crowns what you are doing in the present deeds,
> That all your acts are queens.

(IV.iv.135-146)

We remark about this representation, especially, its powerful suggestion of a greater order or system, in progressive motion, *behind* the re-creative power attributed to Perdita as higher Ego. And it is only on being taken up into this order, active from a realm deep within Nature, that the suffering Ego (represented by Leontes) can hope to find again the integration that, insofar as it is guilty and hopeless, the Ego cannot itself bring about.

On the other hand, the Ego reserves, over time, a direct link and claim to that order's saving power, by virtue of its shame and constant devotion to the memory of the harm that was done, as represented in Leontes:

> Whilest I remember
> Her and her virtues, I cannot forget
> My blemishes in them, and so still think of
> The wrong I did myself...

(V.i.6-9)

That a higher power of Ego can still be positively active here might be taken as an indication that the Ego, in spite of its guilt, still retains a measure of innocence at some level. In a sense this must be true since, from the point of view Shakespeare has established on approaching this play, it is really a matter of a complementary division of the Ego's functions, in innocence and in guilt, enacted *between Pericles* and *The Winter's Tale*.

And so, in going from one play to the other, we imagine what the Ego has already achieved. In its innocence it links up, beyond tragedy, to a higher power in itself. This achievement is *now* brought to bear on the Ego's guilty part. The Ego in its higher power has in the meantime tapped into a still greater Power in Nature which is the principal saving agent here.

By the time we reach the end of *The Winter's Tale*, we may confidently assume, then, a pattern of experience which points to a complete re-integration of the Ego beyond tragedy. That re-integration is the consequence of the activity of a higher power of Ego as well as of Nature, corresponding to an extension of the Consciousness Soul in Imagination and in Inspiration.

In *The Tempest* the pattern is brought to fruition in an experience of Intuition. The whole evolution in Imagination and in Inspiration finds a final focus here *literally* in Prospero's own person who is in some sense, then, Shakespeare himself, since it is his experience that is reflected to us in the progression of these plays.

As Steiner reminds us, Intuition means 'dwelling in God'. [74] Hence the focus here on a concentration of power in the individual 'I' insofar as it finally comes to dwell within the 'I' of God. Consider Prospero's words to Miranda:

> who
> Art ignorant of what thou art, nought knowing
> Of whence *I am,* nor *that I am* more better
> Than Prospero...

(I.ii.17-20)

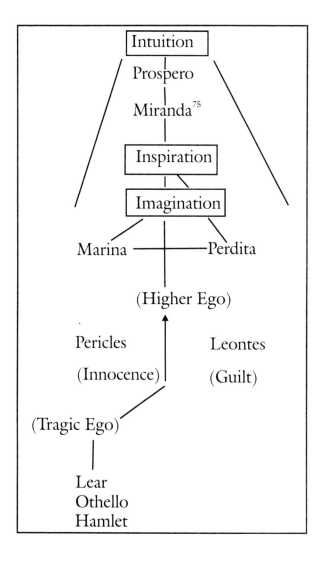

They mediate the words in which God declares Himself (in *Exodus*):

I am that I am...

We thus reach the point where the individual 'I', far beyond the higher relation it has found within itself and within Nature, finally consummates its identity in the God Who dwells within it all.

It was John Middleton Murry who saw in *The Tempest* 'the most perfect prophetic achievement of the Western mind'. 'It stands,' he said, 'on the very verge of a condition that still lies far before the human soul.'[76] But it was typical of the kind of Romantic criticism Murry himself practised. He could have an apprehension of these matters also without any full theory to account for them, or, in his case, any theory at all. Murry's concern rested strictly with *The Tempest* as achievement rather than with the *process* that produced it. For him, Shakespeare finally gathered his strength in *The Tempest* after playing [only] half-wistfully with the figures of his imagination in *The Winter's Tale* [and *Pericles*]'.[77]

Murry could also recognize 'that there are greater and smaller fulfillments', Shakespeare being the greater fulfillment to Romanticism's smaller one.[78] But no more than any other critic working in the Romantic tradition could Murry say precisely how or in what way this was true. Murry could not see what, with the benefit of Anthroposophy, it is possible to see. If it is true, this is because Shakespeare had *already* taken the evolution of the Imagination further — in Inspiration and in Intuition, as far as this was possible in his own time.

It is both ironic and significant that at the time Murry was formulating these views, Steiner had just about completed his great life's work. In him we find a full experience and understanding of the Imagination, Inspiration, and Intuition of which Shakespeare had had his own kind of prophetic experience.

What we have in Shakespeare in outline, as it were, and by suggestion for the most part, is in Steiner for the first time fully presented and accounted for.

Precisely how the Imagination unfolds itself, how it leads on into Inspiration and Intuition, and all that this reveals along the way of a great World-order or system in evolution from ages past down to our own day and beyond into the future — we shall find all duly elaborated upon by Steiner in full and concrete detail. And this is what the 'wisdom' of Anthroposophy represents as a specific content finally accessible to the thinking 'I', apart from the 'wisdom' implied in the process of thinking itself — the two are one for Anthroposophy.[79]

Taking the line which Anthroposophy represents, our approach will be conditioned, at every stage, *by awareness of an astonishingly complex historical evolution*. Thus, among innumerable accounts of that evolution in Anthroposophy, we find the following aimed at substantiating what is happening in the Renaissance (it is itself one of many accounts of that period). Steiner cites a 'power' at that time which

> wants to keep [man], with his consciousness, in spiritual realms that were adapted for him in ancient times. It wants to prevent pure thinking, directed towards the understanding of physical existence, from flowing into his dream-like, imaginative conception of the world.

It is able to hold back, in the wrong way, man's power of perception from the physical world. It is not, however, able to maintain in the right way the experience of the old Imaginations. And so it makes man reflect imaginatively, and yet at the same time he is not able to transplant his soul completely into the world in which the Imaginations have their full value.[80]

Not until the ending of *King Lear* is the process of 'pure thinking' of which Steiner speaks here brought to completion in Shakespeare, to such form of completion as was possible for that time. Before that point, Shakespeare's hero continues to be enmeshed in his 'dream-like, imaginative conception of the world'. Though he is without the right experience of 'the old Imaginations' (for the time for these had passed), nevertheless Shakespeare's hero acts as if he might still be able 'to transplant his soul completely into the world in which the Imaginations have their full value'.

Heroic criticism takes its whole tone and import precisely from awareness of the persistence of an idea of this prospect right through the age in which Shakespeare wrote. Only in *Hamlet*, however, does the hero, in the process of his 'dream-like, imaginative experience', succeed in transplanting himself for a time, and only partially, *into* that [other] world 'in which the Imaginations have their full value'.

Hamlet's vision of the Ghost of his father, in which others also share (namely Marcellus, Bernardo, and Horatio), is precisely such a visually crystallized and objective Imagination. But this vision, which Hamlet is having in the Intellectual or Mind Soul, should be seen as itself signifying merely the latest remnant vision, and among the last, from an earlier time when very much more of an otherworldly nature was revealed. Anthroposophy will indeed confirm that there once

was an otherworldly experience of the very greatest diversification the further back in time we go, and that not so very
long ago (in evolutionary terms) — at the time of the Renaissance, identification with the idea of the possibility of an
otherworldly experience was still great. Among other things,
it was my own independent purpose to show that this was
so in my book, *Otherworldly Hamlet*. But the Consciousness
Soul-experience is at that time in process of accomplishing
through itself a major re-orientation in relation to that idea,
preparing for the accommodation of that new element of
intellectuality or pure thinking with which all otherworldly
experience would, in future, have to contend.

Hamlet marks that point in Shakespeare's imagination
where an otherworldly experience continues to declare itself
in the Intellectual or Mind Soul just as the Consciousness
Soul is coming to birth, so that it *appears* as if an otherworldly
experience can immediately be had again in the Consciousness Soul —though this was not to be for some time yet. By
this I mean that Hamlet anticipates a form of otherworldly
vision that is not just the given or involuntary experience of
the Ghost's earlier and later appearances — the product,that
is, of a relatively 'naive', though supernaturally potent,
thought-life in the Intellectual or Mind Soul. There is the
suggestion that Hamlet also expects a form of vision that
would represent his own individual, fully voluntary possession. This anticipates the production of a far more developed
and higher *Imaginative* thought-life, proceeding out of the
Consciousness-Soul, of the kind that the later Romantics
would themselves come by.

Hamlet stands half-way between the earlier and the
later forms of thought-life, in an unstable relationship to
them both. In fact, it is impossible, at a certain point, to
dissociate Hamlet's anticipation of one form of vision from

an anticipation of the other. The play's ambiguous position in this respect will perhaps justify the approach I make to Hamlet's 'visionary heroism' in *Otherworldly Hamlet*, which represents my own contribution to post-Romantic heroic criticism.

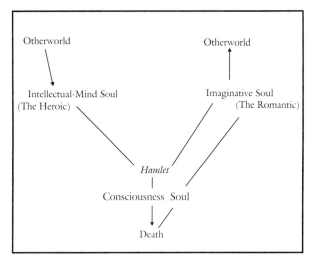

But, in spite of the links between the two in respect of their otherworldly tenor and import, *the 'heroic' and the 'Romantic'* represent substantially different modes, *separated by a major evolution in consciousness*. At least two hundred years of further evolution in the Consciousness Soul stand between Hamlet's own kind of 'Romantic' expectation and that of the later Romantics.

Much, much more would have first to be undergone as regards the consciousness of death. A whole process of alienation would have first to be passed through, in order to effect the right kind of separation from an earlier, otherworldly experience. The consequence of alienation would be: metaphysical disengagement both from the traditional areas of faith (including the area of heroic faith) as well as from more recent, romantic-sensual forms of love (the new 'faith-in-love').

It is precisely this extraordinary 'rite of passage', through what we might call the great 'needle's eye' of the Consciousness Soul-experience, that we find *already* being enacted through and beyond the ending of *King Lear*. Astonishingly, because the full process would not be histori-cally consummated until much later, with the coming of An-throposophy.

With the ending of *King Lear*, we reach the point in Shakespeare's tragic 'progress', as we have seen, of the com-plete negation of all faith, love and life. It has become, by then, entirely a question of the kind and quality of thinking which Shakespeare has brought along with him in meeting the event. With the ending of *King Lear*, we are, indeed, confronted with the whole *problem* of the nature and further possibilities of thinking *in the face of negation*, which Anthro-posophy today will help us to resolve.

There is the case, for instance, of Nicholas Brooke whose instinct and sense for 'pure thinking' led him, alone among his contemporaries, certainly to the right evaluation in assessing the ending of *King Lear*, though he himself would give up hope of understanding any further purpose to the event. Yet it would appear that Brooke was on the right track where he says that to 'stare at the end of the play and nod assent … would be to imagine one's own death' — though Brooke confesses that no more 'than anyone else' could he expect to be able to do this himself. [81]

But here again, it is a question of the way in which imagination is true ('imagining' one's own death). This is to say, the way in which 'thinking' is true, for the experience could hardly be referred to just any kind of cognition or idea of thinking.

It is precisely here that Anthroposophy opens up the way, with the kind of elaborate preparation it offers us in the understanding and experience of thinking. It takes us *through* to the point of that decisive experience where 'the pupil… will need all that presence of mind and faith in the reliability of his path of knowledge which he has had ample opportunity to acquire in the course of his training'.[82]

Coming round to that point, Steiner offers us his own dramatic transposition of the experience which, by analogy, I want to propose Shakespeare in his own way passed through, with and beyond the ending of *King Lear*.

We need to recall that it was for Shakespeare a matter of his assuming, at this point, direct responsibility for the tragedy he had imagined, both from the point of view of innocence and of guilt — a matter, that is to say, of bearing the full burden of tragedy himself.

A further meeting with what Anthroposophy calls 'the Guardian of the Threshold' now takes place, Steiner dramatizing as follows the substance and effect which the Guardian would have in his sudden appearance in Imagination:

> Now all the good and all the bad aspects of your bygone lives are to be revealed to you. Until now they were woven into your own being; they were within you and you could not see them even as with physical eyes you cannot see your brain. But now these aspects release themselves from you; they emerge from your personality. They assume an independent form which you can see, just as you see the stones and plants of the

outer world. And I... am that very Being who has formed a body out of your noble and ignoble doings...

My Threshold is built out of every feeling of fear remaining in you, out of every shrinking from the power to assume full responsibility for *all your deeds and thoughts*. As long as you still have any trace of fear of becoming the director of your own destiny, for just so long does this Threshold lack something that must be built into it. And as long as a single stone is found missing, you must remain at a standstill on this Threshold, as though transfixed; or else you must stumble...

Visible do I stand before you today, as I have ever stood invisible beside you in the hour of death. When you have crossed my Threshold you will enter those kingdoms to which otherwise you had access only after physical death. You now enter them with full knowledge, and henceforth as you move, outwardly visible, about the Earth, you will at the same time move in the kingdom of death... Through me you will die while still living in the body, in order to be reborn into indestructible existence.[83]

At a certain point in the experience of negation, the possibility is given of 'passing' onwards into a new Imaginative life. An otherworldly experience once again takes shape from that same point strictly and entirely as an accomplishment of the Ego-consciousness in thinking. The Ego now builds its own 'threshold' for reaching into that world. It is the purpose and the task of Anthroposophy precisely to provide for the requisite maturing and strengthening of the Ego-consciousness in thinking to ensure that 'passage' into that otherworld is fully and properly accomplished.

In Shakespeare that 'passage' is reflected to us in the first instance as the Imagination of an indestructible existence for the Ego. That existence represents the Ego's new life —

which we have in the form of the figures of Marina, Perdita, and Miranda. For it is the peculiarity of this new world of Imagination that all that is of an inner nature immediately arises in independent, outer form. Hence, the 'allegorical' mode of representation in which the higher experience is given in Shakespeare's romances.

But the experience is far from being as straightforward as it appears. From what Anthroposophy has to say, it assumes the pupil's continual struggle with the Guardian (otherwise known as his *doppelganger* or double) even after this Being gives way to Another Who reveals Himself as the informing and all-controlling Power within these worlds. From here, it is a matter of the student's making himself progressively more familiar with the further experiences in Imagination, Inspiration and Intuition to be known through the help and mediation of the Christ as the great primordial Initiator in the 'passage' from death to new life.

That initiation is made possible today by a certain way of living into one's thinking — amounting to a vocation — which a devoted study of Anthroposophy provides.

We have seen how Shakespeare was led in his own thinking, insofar as the last plays reflect that further evolution to us. What we make of the terms and conditions of these plays will be determined in the end precisely by the extent to which we succeed in *identifying* the kind of initiation-process Shakespeare was passing through at that time. However, it is not my purpose here nor could it be — within the limited scope of this account — to expound any further on the process of initiation. That is a task that we should have to undertake along with Steiner, through the leap into Anthroposophy itself. A full exposition in these terms must await another and fuller approach to the subject, and another day (hopefully in the not too distant future).

It has been my aim here merely to point a path. My intention was to indicate the continuity and the unity for which we should be looking not only in the development of Shakespeare's own work but in that whole history of the evolution of consciousness in which Shakespeare and the Romantic Movement have played a major role.

What I have been seeking in these pages with reference to Anthroposophy, finally, is the vindication of Romantic tradition. Without suggesting that we can or should be satisfied with its achievements or with its modes of comprehension until now, it has seemed to me better to understand how that tradition has evolved and where it was leading, than to seek simply to excise it from our cultural consciousness altogether, as some of our contemporary ideologues suppose they have done already.

The point is not that we have seen the end of Romantic tradition, but that it is only just beginning — though the extreme exclusivity and intolerance of an academic culture that today pretends to egalitarianism in theory may well see to it that a *continuation* is never made.

Uniformity, rather than a diversification of choices — or a dialogue of options — is what today dictates the content of the approach being made to literature at our universities, so that it is unlikely that we shall see for some time yet an approach to literature that would make room for a program of studies on 'Shakespeare and Anthroposophy'. But while we wait, nothing will happen, for it is unlikely that the really new Shakespeare criticism we so desperately need to effect the necessary changes in this direction will come out of the ranks of Anthroposophists themselves, for the Anthroposophical Movement has no special need of it.

The project I propose could only be realized, in fact, if our university doors could open *to* Anthroposophy from without, though the risks in doing so are also great.

For we could only undertake this project with the right intention if, as I have said, we approach the concepts which Anthroposophy yields, prepared at some point to make the further leap into Anthroposophy itself. Anything less than this would mean to allow the tragedy which I spoke of earlier to continue to make headway with us.

Notes

Part One

1. References are to *The Riverside Shakespeare* ed., G. Blakemore Evans (Boston: Houghton Mifflin Co., 1974) unless otherwise stated.

2. See Helen Gardner, 'The Noble Moor', from *Shakespeare's Othello: A Casebook*, ed., John Wain (London: Macmillans, 1971), p.161.

3. 'The Noble Moor', p. 161.

4. Soren Kierkegaard, *Fear and Trembling*. Reference is to the translation by Alastair Hanney (Harmondsworth: Penguin, 1985), p. 65; p. 75.

5. Hanney, p. 90. 'Thanks to you, great Shakespeare!, you who can say everything, everything, everything exactly as it is — and yet why was this torment one you never gave voice to?'

6. See Hiram Haydn, *The Counter-Renaissance* (New York: Harcourt, Brace and World, 1950), especially the chapter 'Elizabethan Romanticism and the Metaphysical Ache', pp. 358-373, where Haydn speaks of an 'expression of will and longing, the denial of limit in the nature of man, and an excessive, insatiate emphasis upon some one value — variously certainty, knowledge, power, honor — that constitutes quite literally a revolt of the ego' (p.367).

7. See David Bevington ed., *Medieval Drama* (Boston: Houghton Mifflin, 1975), p. 308; p. 321.

8. Samuel Johnson, *Johnson on Shakespeare*, ed., Walter Raleigh (London: Oxford University Press, 1959), p. 200.

Part Two

9. Sidney Lanier, *Shakespeare and His Forerunners,* Vol. I, pp. 300-301; cited by Alwin Thaler, *Shakespeare's Silences* (Cambridge, Mass.: Harvard University Press, 1929), pp. 3.

10. A.C. Bradley, *Shakespearean Tragedy* (London: Macmillan Press, 1904), pp. 13-14. See also pp. 19ff.

11. Graham Hough, *A Preface to 'The Faerie Queene'* (London: Gerald Duckworth and Co. Ltd., 1962), p. 107.

12. *A Preface to 'The Faerie Queene'*, p. 105.

13. F. R. Leavis, 'Tragedy and the Medium', from *The Common Pursuit* (London: Chatto and Windus, 1952), p. 130.

14. L. C. Knights, *Some Shakespearean Themes* (London: Chatto and Windus, 1959), p. 23.

15. G. Wilson Knight, *The Wheel of Fire* (London: Methuen and Co. Ltd., 1961; rpt., 1972; orig. pub. Oxford University Press, 1930), p. 11.

16. The general approach and viewpoint outlined here has been thoroughly researched by S. Viswanathan in the context of 'The rise of the poetic interpretation of Shakespeare' in his book *The Shakespeare play as poem* (Cambridge: Cambridge University Press, 1980). My own aim in this book is to set this tradition in criticism back farther than Viswanathan does, though he himself acknowledges at one point that 'The term "incarnation" was originally employed by Wordsworth with reference to poetic language' (p.46 n. 11).

17. Alwin Thaler, *Shakespeare's Silences* (Cambridge, Mass.: Harvard University Press, 1929), p. 12.

18. Blackwood's *1849*, cited by Kenneth Muir in the Arden *Macbeth*, p. 139n.

19. W.H. Clemen, *The Development of Shakespeare's Imagery* (London: Methuen, 1961; first pub., 1951), p. 151.

20. Frank Kermode in his Introduction to the Arden edition of *The Tempest*, p. lxxviii.

21. It is revealing of the representational significance of this action of touching or pointing to the breast to compare what John Bulwer has to say about it in his *Chironomia*, London, 1644: 'The touch doth most availe in a sharpe and inflamed stile, when the motions of the minde are by Action unfolded: As when an Oratour would express an incredible ardour of love lodged in his bosome,

and cleaving to his very marrow; or grief deeply setttled in his yearning bowells...'(pp. 39-40; the symbol 'ſ' for 's' modernized.)

22. For the last line of this speech, I have adopted M.R. Ridley's rendering from the Arden edition of the play.

Part Three

23. '...the very noblest man whom even omnipotence or Shakespeare could ever call to life.' Algernon Swinburne, *A Study of Shakespeare* (New York: AMS Press, 1965), pp. 176-177.

24. James Bulman, *The Heroic Idiom in Shakespearean Tragedy* (Newark: University of Delaware Press, 1985).

25. A tradition that, interestingly, Viswanathan omits to identify and acknowledge in his otherwise thorough survey and review of modern Shakespeare criticism in *The Shakespeare play as poem*. What makes this omission interesting is the indication it offers of Viswanathan's own biased absorption in the form of criticism that opposes itself to this tradition later, as if this tradition, or the opposition to it, had never been. Glossing the situation in this way, Viswanathan misses the occasion to observe the immense significance of this opposition/impasse for the future course of Shakespeare criticism in this century. As I argue below, we were left with a situation that remained *unresolved*, the *whole* situation of modern Shakespeare criticism up to that time falling from that point into disarray, and this from the insufficiency of the general method that had motivated it up till then, that method being, implicitly, the method of Romantic Imagination.

See: Howard Baker, *Induction to Tragedy* (Louisiana: Louisiana State University Press, 1939).

Farnham, Willard. *The Medieval Heritage of Elizabethan Tragedy*. Oxford: Basil Blackwell, 1963; orig. pub., 1936.

Prior, Moody. *The Language of Tragedy*. Bloomington: Indiana University Press, 1947.

Leech, Clifford. *Shakespeare's Tragedies*. London: Chatto and Windus, 1950.

James, D.G. *The Dream of Learning*. London: Oxford at the Clarendon Press, 1951.

Alexander, Peter. *Hamlet: Father and Son*. London: Oxford at the Clarendon Press, 1955.

Bush, Douglas. *Shakespeare and the Natural Condition*. Cambridge, Mass.: Harvard University Press, 1960.

Watson, Curtis. *Shakespeare and the Renaissance Concept of Honor*. Princeton: Princeton University Press, 1960.

Rosen, William. *Shakespeare and the Craft of Tragedy*. Cambridge, Mass.: Harvard University Press, 1960.

Waith, Eugene. *The Herculean Hero*. New York: Columbia University Press, 1962.

Brower, Ruben. *Hero and Saint*. Oxford: Oxford at the Clarendon Press, 1971.

26. *Shakespearean Tragedy*, p. 165.

27. *Shakespearean Tragedy*, pp. 234-235.

28. *The Wheel of Fire*, pp. 221, 236.

29. Barbara Everett, 'The New King Lear', in *Shakespeare's King Lear: A Casebook*, ed., Frank Kermode (London: Macmillan, 1969), pp.187-188.

30. 'On the Tragedies of Shakespeare', from *Lamb's Criticism*, ed., E.M.W. Tillyard (Cambridge: Cambridge University Press, 1923), pp. 45-46.

31. 'The New King Lear', pp. 199-200. Italics mine.

32. Helen Gardner, '*Othello*: A Retrospect, 1900-1967', in *Shakespeare Survey 21*, ed., Kenneth Muir (Cambridge: Cambridge University Press, 1968).

33. At a certain level, of course, both *King Lear* and *Macbeth* are themselves grounded in such qualities of individuality and concentration. In spite of their obviously 'giant' nature, both display and emerge themselves from some 'correspondence with the forms and events of human affairs' (to quote Wilson Knight). Indeed,

without that correspondence, these plays could hardly reflect the way they do upon a vision of human destiny. What is more, the negative comparison of Othello with the later achievements (in point of fact, only two or three years 'later') in respect of power of passion, strikes one as obviously invidious. It has never been doubted that Othello himself is anything less than gigantic. Swinburne, for instance, spoke of the titanic quality of the later Shakespearean tragic heroes and included, of course, his Othello, prized so immemorially, among the list he gives. Bradley himself called attention to something 'colossal' about these same heroes — 'huge men', adding, in his introduction to the subject of the great tragedies, that 'Othello is the first of these men...'

Indeed, a breakthrough had first to be made. That breakthrough once made, we might naturally expect to find progression and evolution, explaining the relatively greater, expanded power of *Lear* and *Macbeth* as creations following immediately on *Othello*.

34. John Bayley, *Shakespeare and Tragedy* (London: Routledge and Kegan Paul, 1981) pp. 8-15 *passim*.

35. T.B. Tomlinson, *A Study of Elizabethan and Jacobean Drama* (Cambridge: Cambridge University Press, 1964).

36. F.R. Leavis, *Education and the University* (London: Chatto and Windus, 1948). L.C. Knights, *Some Shakespearean Themes* (London: Chatto and Windus, 1959).

37. *A Study of Elizabethan and Jacobean Drama*, p.36.

38. *Elizabethan and Jacobean Drama*, p. 27. Tomlinson's passage ends with a quotation from L.C. Knights.

39. Owen Barfield, *Romanticism Comes of Age* (Middletown, Conn.: Wesleyan University Press, 1966), p. 20.

40. *Romanticism*, p. 15.

41. From the thirteenth chapter of the *Biographia Literaria*, ed., James Engell and W. Jackson Bate (Princeton: Princeton University Press, 1983), Vol. I, p. 299. The value of Coleridge's terms can only be grasped, of course, in the context of his entire discussion which begins, and is substantially presented, in the twelfth chapter of the *Biographia*.

42. *Romanticism*, p. 100.

43. *Romanticism*, p. 129-130.

44. Terry Eagleton, *Literary Theory* (Minnesota: University of Minnesota Press, 1983), p. 42. Eagleton's account proceeds in (seemingly deliberate) ignorance of the whole Romantic philosophical tradition and what *it* is making of the 'intuitive'. Coleridge is himself building on that tradition in the definition he offers of the Imagination.

45. F.R. Leavis, *The Living Principle* (London: Chatto and Windus, 1975).

46. From this view, the reader will gather my proposal of a Romantic provenance for the method also of the later 'meta-heroic' critics (rallied here under Leavis' banner), most of whom, among those I cite, Viswanathan (in *The Shakespeare play as poem*) sees as working within a view of the 'poetic interpretation' of Shakespeare that he thinks distinctively modern.

With its 'insistence on "intimations" and indirect suggestions in poetry, and the appeal to faculties other than the conscious' (p.44) and its 'basic presupposition that poetry is a unique mode of discourse, unparaphraseable, especially in rational prose and direct statement' (p.43), Viswanathan acknowledges the possibility of seeing this movement as 'a continuation of the Romantic movement' (p.45). He himself cites the opinion of Frank Kermode (*Romantic Image*) and Graham Hough (*Image and Experience*) to that effect. But he resists this view, claiming that 'as a matter of fact, the ideal hankered after, however difficult in practice, was the co-extensive development, fusion or function in unison of the emotional and the imaginative sensibilities, and of the faculty of reason and judgment' (p.45) .

But it is wrong to assume a desired separation of these functions in the Romantic approach to the Imagination. We are, in any case, on firm ground for dealing with the tragic fortunes of modern Shakespeare criticism in this century (fortunes which Mr. Viswanathan, publishing in 1980, could not really foresee) only by *returning* to the provenance of its major modes in the Romantic method of Imagination. Without that strategy, we have no other way of grasping or approaching the tragedy with any hope of pursuing a solution.

47. 'Austrian-born Rudolf Steiner (1861-1925) became a respected and well-published scholar, particularly known for his work on Goethe's scientific writings. After the turn of the century, he began to develop his earlier philosophical principles into an approach to methodical research of psychological and spiritual phenomena. His multi-faceted genius has led to innovative and holistic approaches in medicine, science, education (Waldorf schools), special education, philosophy, religion, economics, agriculture (the Bio-dynamic method), drama, the new art of eurythmy, and other fields. In l924, he founded the General Anthroposophical Society, which today has branches throughout the world' (from the jacket cover of *Christianity as Mystical Fact* (New York: Anthroposophic Press).

48. *Romanticism Comes of Age*, p.130.

49. *Romanticism*, p.30.

50. *Romanticism*, p.15.

51. *Romanticism*, p.16.

52. *Romanticism*, p. 16.

53. *Romanticism*, p. 37.

54. *Romanticism*, pp. 15-16.

55. Sergei Prokofieff, *Rudolf Steiner and the Founding of the New Mysteries* (London: Rudolf Steiner Press, 1986), p. 72.

56. *Otherworldly Hamlet* (Montreal: Guernica, 1991).

57. *Romanticism*, p. 142.

58. See the account by Hiram Haydn, 'Elizabethan Romanticism and the Metaphysical Ache', from *The Counter-Renaissance*, pp. 358-373: 'On the one hand, an assertive ideal of unlimited freedom, on the other the sense of transiency. And since most of these thinkers and writers among the Elizabethans applied the ideal of unlimited freedom to the limited goods of mortal life — especially the goods of sensuous love and beauty — they were really treating

a naturalistic position with a romanticist attitude. The resultant conflict is everywhere apparent in Elizabethan literature' (p. 61).

59. *Romanticism*, p. 110.

60. *The Wheel of Fire*, p. 140.

61. *The Wheel of Fire,* p. 42.

62. *The Wheel of Fire*, p. 34.

63. *The Wheel of Fire*, p. 28.

64. *The Wheel of Fire*, p.34.

65. See Peter Manns, *Martin Luther: An Illustrated Biography* (New York: Crossroad Publishing Co., 1982), p.180 where Manns speaks of 'The patience and indulgence [Luther] showed his numerous friends, colleagues and brothers who, like Karlstadt, Johann Bugenhagen, Justus Jonas, or Wenzeslaus Link, were suddenly in very much of a rush to extinguish the "burning fire"...' Manns adds that 'it was not Luther who abandoned the monastery, as the mass of his fellow friars did before him and an entire army of monks and nuns did in the sixteenth century... Of course, Luther bears a share of responsibility for this development, but... it is not his fault that monks, nuns, and priests misused the call to "freedom" nor is he the actual cause of this regrettable turn of events.' Manns' conclusion is that 'it was rather that the monastery collapsed around [Luther], as it were. Monasticism was losing its bloom and leaves, like trees in autumn.'

66. Cited by Haydn, *The Counter-Renaissance,* p. 418.

67. See the chapters on 'Sexuality' and 'Revenge' in *Otherworldly Hamlet*.

68. Here I would include Lear along with Hamlet and Othello. The exception to this pattern, of course, is Macbeth in whom an utmost violence is *directly* at work. Its effect in the world of *Macbeth*, nevertheless, is in keeping with the overall pattern. The violence drives one character to acknowledge that 'all is the fear, and nothing is the love' (IV.ii.12). This is not to be seen simply as a failure of moral nature in the characters of the *Macbeth*-world. What *Macbeth* asks us to contemplate is a species of violence, and a degree

of such violence, before which all forms of love, as we know these familiarly, are negated. With *Macbeth* we have moved beyond that point where faith in love is still being tragically affirmed.

69. See above for Johnson's comment on the ending of *Othello*. For his comment on the ending of *King Lear*, see *Johnson on Shakespeare*, pp. 162-163.

70. Nicholas Brooke, 'The Ending of *King Lear*', from *Shakespeare: 1564-1964*, ed., Bloom (Providence, R.I.: Brown University Press, 1964), pp. 86;84.

71. See Bulman, *Heroic Idiom*.

72. Rudolf Steiner, *Christianity as Mystical Fact* (New York: Anthroposophic Press, 2nd edn., 1972), pp. 16-18.

73. The four quotations are from separate sections of Barfield's work: respectively pp. 79-80; p. 98; pp. 101-102; pp. 127-128. I have adjusted Barfield's second diagram to bring this into line with my own diagrams in the rest.

74. Rudolf Steiner, *The Gospel of St. Luke* (London: Rudolf Steiner Press, 3rd edn., 1975), p. 23.

75. Combining both Marina and Perdita, Miranda, in this picture, is the full 'wonder' of the higher world itself, now fully perceived in the Ego.In another sense of her name, Miranda also 'mirrors' this higher world to us: in herself, as literal personage. (The name 'Miranda' contains both senses, of 'wonder' and of 'mirroring'.) At the same time, the world (as we know it) is, in her, 'mirrored' back to us, as it were through the 'eyes' of the higher world. Hence, Miranda's view of the Milan-party: 'O brave new world that hath such people in it.'

76. John Middleton Murry, 'Romanticism and the Tradition', from *Defending Romanticism*, ed., Malcolm Woodfield (Bristol: Bristol Classical Press, 1989), p.142.

77. 'Romanticism and the Tradition', p. 142.

78. 'Romanticism and the Tradition', p. 143: 'In the greater spirits the wheel turns full circle; in the lesser, it turns half or quarter of the way.'

79. In this way, Steiner fulfills the quest for that 'future synthesis' for which Murry, in the essay 'Towards a Synthesis', was looking, back in 1927: 'Objective synthesis is nugatory unless it rests upon a subjective synthesis of which it is the harmonious and orderly projection... Shakespeare's solution, or his system, was simple — it was the re-assertion of tragedy... Not that I suggest that a new synthesis could unfold itself simply through a complete exploration of the implications of Shakespeare's tragedy, considered as experience... my intention is merely to indicate the significance of Shakespeare, and the tragedy which he created, as a symbol and touchstone of a future synthesis. I believe that there will be no essential element in that synthesis that is not implied in Shakespeare; and that, whereas the poetic synthesis of mediaevalism in Dante was subsequent to the philosophic and religious synthesis in St. Thomas, it stands in the very nature of the present epoch that the poetic synthesis should come first and the philosophical synthesis long afterwards' (from *Defending Romanticism*, pp. 196-198).

It is ironic that at the time he was writing these words, Murry should have been ignorant of Steiner, making so much of Shakespeare only because he had not traced out what comes to fulfilment in Steiner. In Theosophy circles in the London of Murry's day, Steiner's name would have been circulating for years if only because he had challenged its structures so radically, and Steiner himself came to London, as the representative of the Anthroposophy he had founded, to lecture just before he died, in 1924. Barfield, I know from firsthand knowledge in an interview I had with him, was among those who had the chance to see Steiner lecture at that time, though there never was a personal meeting between them. It is interesting to note, too, that Yeats was familiar with Theosophy through his wife, and that both may also have known and heard of, and even read, Steiner.

Murry's fate is certainly amongst the most dramatic testimony in our critical history (judging from his words in the passage I cite) of the consequences of limiting our focus strictly to the immediate terms of our activity, whether this be literature, sociology, psychology or history. The need is for a reference point to that further *outside* element that we had failed, or refused, to look into that finally synthesizes all.

80. Rudolf Steiner, *Anthroposophical Leading Thoughts* (London: Rudolf Steiner Press, 1973), p. 108.

81. 'The Ending of *King Lear*', p. 87.

82. See *Knowledge of the Higher Worlds* (London: Rudolf Steiner Press, l969), pp. 191-192.

83. *Knowledge of the Higher Worlds,* pp. 194-195.

Select List of the Works of Rudolf Steiner

The Science of Knowing
Goethean Science
The Philosophy of Freedom
Goethe's World View
Knowledge of the Higher Worlds
Theosophy
Theosophy of the Rosicrucian
The Gospel of St. John
Egyptian Myths and Mysteries
Spiritual Hierarchies
Occult Science
The Gospel of St. Luke
The Gospel of St. Matthew
The Gospel of St. Mark
Building Stones for an Understanding
of the Mystery of Golgotha
World History in the Light of Anthroposophy
Karma Lectures
Anthroposophical Leading Thoughts

A full list may be obtained from the following places:
Rudolf Steiner Press, London.
Anthroposophic Press, Hudson, New York.
Mercury Press, Spring Valley, New York.
Steiner Book Centre, Vancouver.

« L'IMPRIMEUR »

• Cap-Saint-Ignace
• Sainte-Marie (Beauce)
  Québec, Canada
  1996